IT MAY NOT BE YOUR **FAULT**
BUT IT IS YOUR **FIGHT**

CRUSHING
CONDEMNATION

REVISED EDITION

IT MAY NOT BE YOUR **FAULT**
BUT IT IS YOUR **FIGHT**

CRUSHING CONDEMNATION

TERESA VERDECCHIO

Ridley Park, Pennsylvania

CRUSHING CONDEMNATION

© 2015-2021 Teresa Verdecchio.

Published by Teresa Verdecchio | Ridley Park, PA

Previous Edition ISBN: 978-0-98610510-4

New Edition ISBN (Print): 978-1-7352777-0-7

ISBN (Kindle): 978-1-7352777-1-4

Library of Congress Control Number (LCCN): 2020911453

Printed in the United States of America

Prepared for Publication: www.wendykwalters.com

To contact the author: www.newdestinychristiancenter.com

DEDICATION

This book is lovingly dedicated to my husband,
the man I call King David.
You have walked with me through it all,
continually modeling the unconditional love of Father God.
I love doing life with you.

This book is also dedicated to my children,
Hannah, Jonathan, and Lisa.
May you live every day knowing that you are fiercely loved.

ACKNOWLEDGMENT

A special thank you to Wendy Walters and Palm Tree Productions for all your guidance and expertise with this project. Your kindness and patience helped me learn so much during this transformative journey.

PRAISE FOR CRUSHING CONDEMNATION

Condemnation is one of the enemy's greatest weapons used against God's people. It creates a sense of failure, self-hatred, starting and stopping, religious performance, etc. It's like a strong claw that violently grips our hearts and refuses to let go. In *Crushing Condemnation*, Teresa Verdecchio unmasks this destructive tool that is so craftily used to hinder God's people from walking in the freedom that we are granted in Christ. With unbridled transparency, Teresa reveals the steps of her path and shows through personal experience what it means to walk in liberty. She also illuminates our identity in Christ and points the way to glorious intimacy with Him that leads to true righteousness. This book is a powerful roadmap that will be used to release many from the demonic influence of condemnation. Read it repeatedly and allow the truths contained within to set you free!

—KEITH COLLINS
Founder of Generation Impact Ministries | keith-collins.org
Founder of Impact Global Fellowship | impactgf.org
Host of "Maintain the Flame" Podcast | Charisma Podcast Network | iTunes

Condemnation is an emotional trap the enemy of our soul ensnares us with and then sets the cruise control of self-destruction that we cannot humanly cancel. But God, by His grace, can intercept our downward spiral. In writing *Crushing Condemnation*, Teresa Verdecchio has revealed her journey's waypoints and major points. She humbly utilizes transparency, masterful verbiage, and powerful scriptural truths. She shows how one travesty can propagate a life-long revolving door of trials. Yet, her story did not end in the "loop" of defeat. The Holy Spirit led her into liberty, transformation, and God-inspired progress. The finished product was condemnation no longer doing the crushing, but condemnation being CRUSHED in a Spirit-led process fueled by His overcoming grace. This work will be a resource to lead people into Christ's "INDEED" freedom

—TIM HODGE
Crossroads World Outreach Center | cwoconline.org
Husband, Dad, Author, Minister, Chairman of the Barnabas Forum, Executive Council
Member of the S.C. Conference International Pentecostal Holiness Church

viii | CRUSHING CONDEMNATION

After reading *Crushing Condemnation*, I feel compelled to honor the author, Teresa Verdecchio, for sharing her life experiences, which led her to the revelation that condemnation was the enemy seeking to destroy her. Her motivating factor in writing this book was so that others could read and be free! It takes a COURAGEOUS act of your WILL to SURRENDER, and CHOOSE to NOT stay in your WOUNDED PLACE but SEEK DIVINE TREATMENT and ALLOW HIM to do whatever it takes to make you WHOLE! Teresa has made this courageous move, and I say thank you!

—DIANE MULLINS
Founder of Deborah's Voice | dvmovement.org
Co-Pastor of Calvary Church in Hamilton, Ohio
Conference Speaker

As a senior pastor, I see first hand how condemnation paralyzes the lives of believers. Condemnation is like a demonic security blanket. You know it has to go, but you can't imagine living without it. *Crushing Condemnation* has the answers for which you so desperately need. Pastor Teresa Verdecchio takes us with her on the journey from living under condemnation every single moment of every single day, to complete and total freedom. With vulnerable transparency, she shares the horrific events which led to the stronghold of condemnation taking root in her life and clearly outlines the steps she took to receive deliverance. I can't wait for the people of my church to get their hands on this book! Read *Crushing Condemnation* to change the course of your entire life and help you fulfill your destiny in Jesus!

—DR. JAMIE MORGAN
Senior Pastor of Life Church in Williamstown, NJ
Host of "Fire Starter with Dr. Jamie Morgan" Podcast | iTunes
Author of *My Journal to Ministry: Discover Your Calling,
Purpose, and Destiny* | jamiemorgan.com

Teresa Verdecchio wrote *Crushing Condemnation* authentically and full of vulnerability to bring freedom and healing to its readers. This book is powerful—spiritually and practically. Whether the reader is looking for healing or knows someone who needs healing, these pages are laced with the empowerment of the Holy Spirit to overcome. Encouragement, bravery, and liberty are found between its pages. Read and prepare yourself for a journey to face condemnation and win.

—HEATHER SCHOTT
Lead Pastor of Mercy Culture Church in Fort Worth, TX | mercyculture.com
Founder of The Justice Reform | thejusticereform.com
Author of *Unscarred* | unscarredbook.com

You will be different one year from today because of two things: the people you associate with and the books you read. Both of these things open our eyes and our lives to information that changes the way we think and act. Some books are full of information. This book, however, is able to impart revelation into your spirit that can bring healing to your soul. The study guide used in conjunction with this book is a vital part of the healing process and when applied, will be used in preparation for your divine assignment. Teresa Verdecchio has walked through the pages of this book with one hand on her pen, and the other hand held tight to Father God. She allows herself to be vulnerable so that others can receive the freedom she so desperately sought. She speaks with the heart of a true pastor who has a deliverance anointing, combined with the prophetic insight from the Holy Spirit that comes from a woman who is a radiant example of what she preaches. She crushes condemnation and knows that even though it is not her fault, it is her fight! It is your fight too, and with these tools, you can win!

—RENA PEROZICH
Pastor of MFC Ministries, Inc. in Morgantown, WV | restorationchurchintl.org
Founder of Women of Witness | womenofwitnessministries.org
Author of *Moments That Matter*
Columnist for *Jubilee Magazine*
The Remarkable Blog | RPMDaily.net

All of us are broken. Even those who appear to have it all together are or have been broken. Each of us has weak areas where the enemy of our souls applies enough pressure to exploit that fragility and wrap enough deception around truth to leave us feeling unworthy, unfaithful, or unloved—condemned. In religious circles where we have rightfully been taught how to "take thoughts captive," don the "full armor of God," and walk in "the peace that passes understanding," it can be difficult to admit areas where we need healing, let alone confront them. Teresa Verdecchio has been there and done that. It was hollow. It was a form of godliness that denied the power, rendering her church-culture acceptable without the freedom that comes from true heart transformation. That journey has led her to write *Crushing Condemnation* and its *Companion Study Guide.* Her passion for wholeness and connection to the Father without filters in between has compelled her to share her process with you.

—WENDY K. WALTERS
Friend, Safe Place, Freedom Champion
The Favor Foundation | favorfoundation.org
Executive Coach, Author, and Motivational Speaker | wendykwalters.com
Ghostwriter, Editor, Author & Publishing Coach | palmtreeproductions.com

CONTENTS

xiii   INTRODUCTION

CHAPTER 1
1   CONDEMNATION CULPRIT

CHAPTER 2
9   RECOGNIZE THE ENEMY

CHAPTER 3
17   MIND BATTLES

CHAPTER 4
23   THE ROOT OF THE MATTER

CHAPTER 5
33   GOD'S FATHER HEART

CHAPTER 6
43   FACED WITH GRACE

CHAPTER 7
51   COVERED BY LOVE

CHAPTER 8
61   RENEWING THE MIND

CHAPTER 9
71   AN ESSENTIAL TRUTH

CHAPTER 10
79   MOVING FORWARD

CHAPTER 11
89   BEAUTY FROM THE ASHES

97   EPILOGUE

103   ABOUT THE AUTHOR

INTRODUCTION

As I reviewed this manuscript to add new insights and refresh the content, the world is crashing. The Corona Virus hit, causing the stock market to plummet and millions of people to lose their jobs resulting in record-high unemployment. The country is ordered to shelter in place inside our homes in order to "flatten the curve," which is an attempt to make sure our health care system can cope with the rate at which people get this highly contagious virus. Fear is in the air. We watch a ticker on the news depicting the number of new cases reported and how many people have died each day. Everything we knew about the world just a few short weeks ago has changed overnight.

If the virus was not enough, the country faced several high-profile police killings which led to protests, rioting, looting, and destruction in cities across the nation. The political climate was tense, with hearings for a new and conservative Supreme Court Justice, an upcoming and tense election season with eventual allegations of extreme fraud, and continued lockdowns of businesses going into the holiday season. People were on edge.

An invisible bully showed up to change our lives and wreak havoc in our society. It happened in a moment. Suddenly. But isn't that how a bully works? When a bully sets their sights on you, they begin to terrorize you for no reason other than malevolent mischief.

COVID 19 is a global pandemic, unleashing fear, anxiety, and panic. In America, we saw a run on stores resulting in shortages of food, paper products, and cleaning products. In densely-populated areas, fights broke out as people scrambled to hoard basic supplies. Churches, bars, and schools closed. The entertainment industry shut down. Sports were sidelined, and social distancing became the new norm.

Globally, people cried out for relief, wanting everything to go back to normal—the way things were before this virus viciously attacked us. If only it were that simple, if only we could turn back the clock, hit reset, and start over as if nothing terrible happened.

I cannot find fault with the world for wanting to return to what was once normal. My whole childhood was spent chasing the same thing. I wanted nothing more than a chance to return to *that* day and get back my innocence. Somehow, if I could go back in time and change that moment, it might silence that vitriolic voice that tormented me.

> I WANTED NOTHING MORE THAN A CHANCE TO RETURN TO *THAT* DAY AND GET BACK MY INNOCENCE

We are still in the throes of the pandemic as I write. We do not yet have a vaccine. There is no trusted treatment protocol yet in place, and the faith the world held that 21st Century medicine had made us invincible was shattered. We are coming to terms with our vulnerability.

I believe nothing will be quite the same after the Corona Bully is escorted from the global schoolyard. But as I sit here, quarantined from the world, I am hiding in a place that took me a long, long time to find—even after I knew the way to it. I knew it in theory, but it would take me some time before I experienced it in practice.

You see, I know what it is to be a victim of a bully. Just as the Corona Virus is bullying the whole earth and has demanded the disruption of our lives, I was bullied by condemnation. That bully shoved me around and dictated how I would live for many years.

I am sheltered in the Secret place of the Most High God. I have found a new shadow under His wing, and it is unlike the dark shadow that left me devastated with shame. Here, in the shadow of the Almighty, I have learned to run to God as my refuge and let the storms pass.

It is my prayerful hope that this book will become a friend, the brave defender of truth, a bold reminder of who you really are in Christ—the fearfully, wonderfully, unique, one-of-a-kind, brilliant being you were created to be before the enemy came and breached your life ...

THE VOICE OF THE ACCUSER

From the outside, everything looked fine. I had health, a great marriage, a stable family, and a solid ministry. But what most people did not know was that I suffered from a constant barrage of negative thoughts and emotions continually. This mental state started early in childhood and continued for decades.

I had learned enough from some great faith teachers not to confess everything I was feeling, so the inner battle raged on privately. After all, what good would it do just to sit around, murmuring and complaining? I kept a fairly decent confession, but something had to give. Something had to change. I couldn't live this way any longer. For me to be able to go further in life, I needed to conquer and silence the bullying voice of condemnation. For the constant condemning, internal chatter was fueling destructive actions and cycles that were affecting my present and had the potential to destroy my future.

Thankfully by God's grace, I was able to ferret out the entry point when condemnation entered my life.

When I was five years old, I received Jesus as my personal Lord and Savior. The experience was so real, and for being so young, I just got it! I believed that Jesus loved me, died on the cross for me, and had a place for me in heaven. I was so happy that I was saved. Later on, at the age of seven, I was water baptized. I loved Jesus so much. Telling others about Him and leading them to Him was part of my life, even at a young age.

I felt very close to Jesus and encountered His presence. He would speak to me, and whatever burdens I felt on my heart, I would take them to Him in prayer. It was not uncommon to find me in my room reading my Bible and memorizing scripture. Not that I was trying to memorize them, I would read them, and they just stuck in my brain. I loved church, and I even felt the call to preach at a very young age. I knew the hand of God was on my life. But that was all about to change.

It was a hot summer day in Arizona at the tender age of eight. I was lured to a shady area under a pine tree and sexually violated. What the perpetrator left on my soul was far more damaging than what he did to my body. He did something to my mind that was devastating. This personal experience sowed seeds of condemnation that would take root and sprout weeds that would choke everything healthy and fruit-bearing in my life. Up to that point, my trust in God was simple and childlike.

I WAS LURED TO A SHADY AREA UNDER A PINE TREE AND ...

Since my first release of this book, there was an explosion of the #MeToo movement that saw powerful perpetrators who prowled for prey undeniably exposed. In an instant, the tables were turned, and arrogant offenders were left hiring attorneys to try to stay out of jail. Their guilt was plastered everywhere, as the scandal of their sexual shame led the headlines for weeks. In some high profile cases, justice has been served, and sentences handed down. It is ironic how the perpetrators were placed in a penitentiary when they had little regard for those they put in a mental prison.

After that day, under that pine tree, I began serving what felt like decades of a life sentence with Condemnation as my warden and Shame and Reproach as my correction officers.

For years, I would beat myself up. There was a voice repeatedly accusing me, saying things like:

"Why did you let him talk you into going under that tree?"

"Why didn't you say NO!"

"Why didn't you scream?"

"Why couldn't you make him stop?"

"Why didn't you hide from him?"

"Why did you like it?"

"Why do you hate him? After all, it is wrong to hate someone!"

"What if your mom found out?

"What if your dad knew?"

"You better not tell anyone … remember what he said?!"

"God is mad at you."

"God hates you."

"If the rapture happened, you would not go."

"You are dirty."

"You are spoiled."

"You are filthy."

"You better try to be good and not get in any more trouble!"

The violation of this villain took place in the shadows. The light was blocked by thick, overlapping branches of dense pine needles, and these created a cover for his evil to be carried out in secret. This set in motion a pattern of how I would live after that defiling day—not in the light but in shadows, in concealed places, covered by shameful secrets driven by a desire to be good and perfect, but also with a need to feed something that was awakened before its time.

The most heartbreaking thing from that demonic day was the damage it put between that little girl—me—and her God. This resulted in a painful journey of trying to get God to love me …

I realize that not everyone will relate to my story. After all, it exposes the dark inner dialogue of a person trapped in the cellar of condemnation. It reveals a monster living within that is a cruel taskmaster. I rejoice that there are people who do not struggle in this area. I'm married to such a man. He has provided me with great inspiration and stability. We have completely opposite backgrounds, and though this was not his battle, he has walked through it with me.

I have discovered just how many people, like me, battle condemnation and struggle with believing or feeling the love of Father God. These souls have typically been wounded and have backgrounds of abuse in some manner or another. I have counseled, encouraged, and prayed for some of them in my travels. I'm writing this book in the hope of helping many of them escape the continual cries of, "You're not good enough. You're a failure, a disappointment, guilty, and will never succeed!"

This book shares some of my journey in the hopes of helping others get free. I think it's time that we quit pretending things aren't as dark inside and turn on the light. It's time we emerge from the secrecy of this life of torment. I don't know that world peace is attainable, but I do know that inward peace is. God's Word cannot lie.

IT'S TIME THAT WE QUIT PRETENDING THINGS AREN'T AS DARK INSIDE AND TURN ON THE LIGHT

It is my prayerful hope that this book will become a friend, the brave defender of truth, a bold reminder of who you really are in Christ—the fearfully, wonderfully, unique, one of a kind brilliant being before the enemy came and breached your life ...

The Kingdom of God is righteousness, peace, and joy in the Holy Ghost (Romans 14:17). I am not content to live without it. May God bind His peace over you as you discover the righteousness Jesus came to give us. It surely shall result in joy.

CONDEMNATION CULPRIT

There is therefore now no condemnation to them which are in Christ Jesus, who walk not after the flesh, but after the Spirit.

ROMANS 8:1, KJV

Why do I often hear from countless sons and daughters of God who are doing their best to please God and yet feel they fall short? How do we get our theology to match our reality? How do we live what the Bible promises us in regards to abundant life? If we are in Christ and there is no condemnation for those who walk according to the Spirit and not the flesh, then why did I live in a continual state of condemnation for the majority of my life?

These questions gnawed at me. I knew that freedom from this torment was available and possible. I witnessed it displayed within others. They exuded confidence in their walk with God that emanated peace. Having figured out the reason for the deep pit of condemnation in which my mind dwelt, I desperately sought to be free. But it was some time before I would experience it.

What, after all, is the definition of condemnation?

CONDEMNATION: The act of condemning; the judicial act of declaring one guilty, and dooming him to punishment.[1]

CONDEMN: 1) To pronounce to be utterly wrong; to utter a sentence of disapprobation against; to censure; to blame. But the word often expresses more than censure or *blame* and seems to include the idea of utter rejection; as, to condemn heretical opinions; to *condemn* one's conduct. 2) To determine or judge to be wrong, or guilty; to disallow; to disapprove. 3) To witness against; to show or prove to be wrong, or guilty, by a contrary practice. 4) To pronounce to be guilty; to sentence to punishment; to utter sentence against judicially; to doom; opposed to *acquit* or *absolve*; with *to* before the penalty. 5) To doom or sentence to pay a fine.[2]

Understanding what we are up against is vital in overcoming condemnation. For the war is not waged in the external world, but rather in the inner recesses of the mind. Imagine condemnation manifested and woven deep into your inner dialogue, driven by a strong self-hatred, and you will get an inkling of the internal storm that raged within me.

RECOGNIZING THE VOICE OF CONDEMNATION

Let's go back to the day under the pine tree when I was violated and my innocence was stripped. Immediately, the thoughts screamed in my head, *"You're going to hell! If the rapture comes, you will be left behind! You are bad! God is mad at you!"*

I remember how painful the words were as they resonated in my head and how they crushed me. They literally hurt my heart. Somehow I felt like it must have been my fault even though I was a child, a defenseless child. From that moment on, I struggled inside to get God just to like me again. I tried to recapture that world I knew with Jesus before that life-altering day—the day that left me feeling isolated.

This terrible secret was something that I kept hidden for a long time. I told no one about the event until nearly twenty years later. By then, the damage almost felt irreversible as the tone of condemnation was so familiar, and my voice had become one with it. A steady diet of condemning internal voices was enough to get in the way of me functioning at my full potential. It came to the point where my inner self-talk had reached critical mass. I felt wrong all the time, not just that I did wrong but that I was wrong—my very being. The noise in my head was continual and incessant.

I FELT WRONG ALL THE TIME, NOT JUST THAT I DID WRONG BUT THAT I WAS WRONG—MY VERY BEING

Discovering that others battle this internal whirlwind of condemnation solidifies my belief that this is not uncommon. Living in a world where your worth is continuously reduced to nothing, it seems better to hide than expose it for everyone to see. You become familiar with internal dialogue like, *You're no good! You stupid idiot, don't you know anything?* You drive yourself to perform to the never-ending tune of: *You need to try harder, do better. What have you done? Why did you do it that way? What were you thinking?*

There is a pervasive feeling that you will never measure up to the standard, that you're a failure, and you might as well just quit. So you tell yourself lies and adopt a defeatist attitude. *Nothing is ever good enough; just quit now before you make a fool of yourself.* In that place, it is common to hear taunting thoughts like these: *If you're not going to do it right, then don't do it at all! It's my fault. I am to blame! I must have done something wrong.* This berating dialogue leaves one feeling forever condemned and can lead to erroneous conclusions such as, *I'm the reason why they left.*

For some people, the struggle is not as severe as others. But certain tell-tale signs can help you recognize if you are prone to condemnation. When you can easily blame and put yourself down, constantly berate your efforts, give yourself backhanded dismissals, and think that nothing is ever good enough. When you angrily attack yourself with statements like, *I'm stupid, fat, worthless, less than or bad*—these words may be another sign that you deal with this spirit. A good clue that condemnation plagues you is when the voice that drives you to irrationally try harder, go farther, be stronger, and do better, is one of strong disapproval. These words wound you, and they are as hurtful as the condemning tone that judges you.

CONDEMNATION VS. CONVICTION

Distinguishing the voice of God from that of condemnation was a challenge. But making that distinction is necessary for freedom. There is a difference between conviction and condemnation. Too many want to ignore the voice of our dear and close friend, the Holy Spirit, who convicts us when we do something wrong, sin, or make mistakes. We feel bad, so we run and hide due to shame. The purpose of conviction is to get us to repent and receive forgiveness so we can move on without anything between God and us. It keeps the relationship pure.

Conviction is a gift. It is the friend of repentance that leads us to a cleansed conscience and soul. The moment we repent, conviction lifts, and peace is restored in relationship with God, our Father. Conviction is uncomfortable but never abusive and critical. That is not how the Holy Spirit speaks to us.

Condemnation is destructive as it makes us feel hopeless and condemned. It sets up our minds to refuse the truth of the Word and believe the faulty lie. Often condemnation blinds one to any strengths they have, all they can see are the weaknesses. It distorts thinking. We become blind and do not see as God sees. It robs us of overflowing joy.

God does not speak condemnation to His children. It is never the voice of God, ever! Paul clearly stated this truth: "There is therefore now no condemnation to them which are in Christ Jesus" (Romans 8:1). Will we muster the courage to believe and live it? Ricardo Sanchez summed it up well when he said, "The devil knows your name but calls you by your sin. God knows your sin but calls you by your name." Conviction brings the realization that restoration and redemption are possible, while condemnation offers no such hope.

EXAMINING THE BITTER FRUIT OF CONDEMNATION

Fostering a mindset that is laden with condemnation essentially traps the mind in a cycle that yields the same result: failure. That is, failure to really live. Abundant life seems as elusive as a pot of gold at the end of the rainbow. What becomes familiar is a life filled with the following, capturing the mind in a seemingly endless pit.

Following is a sample of the fruit of condemnation:

- **LOW SELF-ESTEEM**: The focus was on self and all my inferiorities and failures resulting in self-hatred, self-judgment, self-loathing, accompanied by self-blame, with an urge to often say "I'm sorry" whether I did anything wrong or not.

- **PERFECTIONISM**: Doing things perfectly all the time was very important because errors and failures brought condemnation and pain. To avoid the agony, I was driven to perform, earn it, and be good enough. Silliness and frivolous activities were annoyances to me. Relax? No way! That's how one gets behind. Rest? That's for lazy folks, and that was not me! My nose was usually stuck in how-to books as I strove to have a sober mindset. Perfectionism and condemnation are close cousins, so one feeds off the other. It's a definite killjoy where the creative child within is suppressed.

- **RIGIDITY**: Fun was rarely a part of my vocabulary. "Put your hand to the plow" was my motto. Condemnation effectively robbed me of joy, laughter, and being present so I could fully celebrate the moment. Fortunately, the people that I did life with loved me regardless of my inability to enjoy the life I'd been given with them.

- **UNDERACHIEVER**: As ridiculous as it sounds, I was comfortable to a degree, in the confines of condemnation. It rendered me inoperable in some seasons so that it was okay for me not to reach my potential. That was my crutch. This was also my excuse to go ahead and be a failure and to underachieve. The truth was that I was afraid of success.

I knew how to fail quite well, but I didn't know how to succeed. It paralyzed my potential and made it inevitable that I would avoid doing the stuff that scared me.

- **INSECURITY:** When I was not secure in my person, genuinely believing that I was accepted, loved, wanted, and that I actually did belong, then I was capable of doing just about anything to find security. Many of us could tell horror stories of what we did or said in our attempt to be accepted.

Condemnation is both a killer and a crutch. I cringe at the years that I lost using it as an excuse to stay in comfort. I knew what the Word of God stated regarding me, but as much as I loved Jesus, I lacked the revelation of what it truly meant to be a daughter of God. The thought of a loving Father who was fond of me was ludicrous. I felt I had to earn everything and struggled to receive anything. The problem with that belief, as I later discovered, is that everything in this walk with God is all about receiving. We cannot earn a thing.

ENDNOTES

1. "condemnation." http://webstersdictionary1828.com/ Dictionary/condemnation, 2020. Web 05 May 2020.

2. "condemn." http://webstersdictionary1828.com/ Dictionary/condemn, 2020. Web 05 May 2020.

CONDEMNATION IS BOTH A KILLER
AND A CRUTCH. IT BLINDS US TO ANY
STRENGTHS WE HAVE, PREVENTS US FROM
SEEING OURSELVES AS GOD SEES US,
AND ROBS US OF OVERFLOWING JOY.

RECOGNIZE THE ENEMY

*The thief comes only in order
to steal and kill and destroy.*

JOHN 10:10 AMP

We have an enemy. He is called the devil for a good reason, and he comes for one thing—destruction. His resume clearly states that he comes to steal, kill, and destroy. He likes to operate by stealth, remaining undetected for as long as possible. Taking advantage of a person's mind that is captured by condemnation is not very surprising. He authors the condemning and accusing thoughts that run rampant in the mind, and so he is rightly called the "the accuser of the brethren."

And I heard a loud voice saying in heaven, "Now is come salvation, and strength, and the kingdom of our God, and the power of his Christ: for the accuser of our brethren is cast down, which accused them before our God day and night."

REVELATION 12:10 KJV

Notice the difference. While the devil accuses us day and night before the throne, Jesus ever lives to make intercession for us.

Therefore He is also able to save to the uttermost
those who come to God through Him, since He
always lives to make intercession for them.

HEBREWS 7:25 NKJ

Here is no shocking news flash: Sin causes condemnation. Habitual sin can intensify it. And if we do not close the door and lock the windows, the devil will look for access into our lives. Listening to the lies of condemnation provides a wide-open door. Shut the door on the devil and latch the windows. The devil needs a passive will and a blank mind to go to work.

KNOWING THE ENEMY

As a child and young Christian, I had no idea about spiritual warfare. There was an assault on many fronts in my life. Under condemnation, not only is there an attack on the mind, but demonic strongholds are built due to a certain way of thinking over a long time. It is a belief empowered by strong emotions. These are strongholds built around the lies that have wounded us.

The one event in my childhood that took my innocence bled deep into my life as I matured. Due to shame, I judged myself as different, less-than, worthless, and pitiful, and that became a stronghold in my mind. Consequently, the new world that had been awakened in me as a child would lead to a cycle of sin, condemnation, conviction, repentance, and sin again and again. I recall even in my teen years hearing relentless condemning thoughts running through my mind. They were harrowing accusatory statements. It was a torturous prison, with mental bars as strong as any steel ones in a prison.

Not fully grasping the truth, the enemy took advantage of my naivety. With a mind that was beating me up constantly with critical self-analysis, I spent years loving God but running from Him. I was ashamed. I hid in hyper-religious activity and worked really hard for His acceptance. After I felt I paid enough of a price and performed well enough, I would sheepishly approach His throne of grace. Forget about the come boldly part, I cowered.

> Let us then fearlessly and confidently and boldly draw near to the throne of grace (the throne of God's unmerited favor to us sinners), that we may receive mercy [for our failures] and find grace to help in good time for every need [appropriate help and well-timed help, coming just when we need it].
>
> HEBREWS 4:16 AMP

Riddled with insecurities that I was not accepted, loved, and forgiven because I screwed up, I avoided God. It took time for me to understand that when I sin, I can run to Him and not from Him.

CONFRONTING THE SEXUAL ISSUE

This was a major area that I had to deal with in my quest for freedom. It is a breeding ground for condemnation. Certainly, for me, this was true. As a victim of childhood sexual abuse and as one who struggled in this area throughout my teen years, the battle ensued because it was no longer due to victimization but to choice. I believe sexual immorality is very destructive. It certainly is a sin against our own bodies and a sin against self.

Despite a culture where anything goes, and the push to normalize all sexual behavior, the Bible still declares that all sexual immorality is sin. This clamor of culture simply does not help in the area of condemnation. Sure, in the midst of fleshly gratification, we abandon ourselves to the temporary and fleeting pleasures of sin. Still, an honest person will tell you that afterward, there is guilt and condemnation. Usually, it doesn't quite turn out the way Hollywood and society said it would. Many are left with conflicting thoughts such as *Why do I feel dirty inside? That was not what I thought it would be!*

As a child, I hated how I felt after someone misused my body. Unfortunately, sexual abuse became a recurring theme after that fateful day. Hiding in my good performance because I felt so bad about myself was my defense against such feelings. I worked hard to prove that I wasn't as bad as I felt. The problem was that when I wasn't working or performing well, I felt terrible.

A cycle of condemnation was set in me early through the abuse, and soon I started volunteering for the behavior. Consequently, that only deepened the issue resulting in much oppression and depression. Giving in to sin led to bouts of condemnation. One fed the other. Feeling bad only drove me to do the very thing that was causing the condemnation. Afterward, I would try to behave because I acted out/sinned. Without fail, I would beat myself up and vowed to change, followed by trying my best to be good. Eventually, I couldn't keep up with the perfectionism and the unrealistic demands I had for myself; the pressure would mount and drive me to the secret sin again. The miserable and vicious cycle would start again. It was a trap, and at times I felt hopeless. I hated my life, and I loathed the cycle. We are as sick as our secrets, and my soul was very sick.

> WE ARE AS SICK AS OUR SECRETS, AND MY SOUL WAS VERY SICK

To those of you who are in the sin cycle, there is a method to the devil's madness. He entices and tempts you to do the very things that you hate, and when you fall, he is there to accuse you for doing it. He will bait you to do it and then ensnare and mock you. The name devil means accuser. His mission is to slander and defame. If he is talking, he is accusing. Undoubtedly, he will be there to tell you how you are no good and how God hates you. I beg to differ. If you just muster the courage and take the dark and shameful thing to Jesus, and let His perfect love cast out the fear of those wounded places, then the healing will come. Jesus longs to touch the wounded places in our soul, whether it is a memory, imagination, trauma, or event that left us scarred.

STOPPING THE CHASE

I loved God with all my heart and was obsessed with wanting more of Him. I didn't want this tormenting force to exist in the most important relationship in my life. I was not content to live confined in condemnation. The Lord reminded me of a situation years ago when my daughter was young.

Growing up, my daughter was surrounded by boys, her younger brother, and two boy cousins. You know how little boys are with little girls or their sisters! They would continually tease and chase her. There were three of them running after her all in the name of fun. She would run, get tired, and then cry.

One day she ran to me and complained about the boys chasing her. I bent down and whispered in her ear, "Don't run! If you don't run, they can't chase you!" Her eyes widened as a smile crossed her little face at the revelation.

Sure enough, the gang of boys found her soon after, and she instinctively started to run. But then she suddenly stopped. The stunned look on the boys' faces was priceless because they didn't know what to do. They looked around, lost. She had changed the game on them. That was the last day they ever chased her.

I think condemnation is like that. It will chase us just for the sheer fun of it. We merely need the revelation that if we don't run, it can't chase us! What I had to do was stop running from deep internal things (mainly memories) that were the root causes of the condemnation. Taking that step was critical. There is an active decision we make not to allow condemnation to chase us. In stopping the run, we can learn to dance. I'd rather dance with the Holy Spirit than to be chased by condemnation's cohorts.

We typically are okay with God when we feel like we are behaving. It is when we feel so broken and are a stinking mess that in our pain, we run to a counterfeit for comfort only to realize that it made it worse. At that moment, our Father is inviting us to come to Him and not to run away. It is as if He is saying, "Just come; bring it here, bring it to the light. Let Me touch that place and don't hide it from Me, but bring it to Me and let Me heal and restore you." Responding to His call takes courage. But if you can get there and if you can see His eyes of love, He is not screaming at you that you are bad. Jesus took your place on the cross, and the wrath of God was satisfied through the sacrifice of the blood of Jesus.

However, we must repent for any sin committed. We must meet the conditions of God's instructions in the Bible. We are first to humble ourselves and repent. We must confess and forsake our sin. Our merciful Savior is faithful and just to forgive us of all sin and cleanse us of all unrighteousness.

> If we confess our sins, He is faithful and just to forgive
> us our sins and to cleanse us from all unrighteousness
>
> 1 JOHN 1:9 NKJV

Repentance is a vital step to fully embracing the reconciliation and restoration provided by Jesus' finished work.

ENDNOTE

1. Devil 1228. Diabolos: slanderous, accusing falsely (From 1225/diaballo, to slander, accuse, defame.) *Strong's Concordance of the Bible.*

GIVING IN TO SIN WILL LEAD TO BOUTS OF
CONDEMNATION, ONE FEEDING THE OTHER, DRIVING
YOU TO DO THE VERY THINGS CAUSING YOU SHAME.

THE DEVIL NEEDS A PASSIVE WILL
AND A BLANK MIND TO GO TO WORK.
RESIST HIM AND HE MUST FLEE.

BROKEN AND BRUISED, RUN TO THE FATHER.
CONFESS YOUR SINS, AND BE CLEANSED.

MIND BATTLES

Let this mind be in you which was also in Christ Jesus.

PHILIPPIANS 2:5 KJV

What do I do when my living condition does not match my legal position? There are positional truths in the Word of God, Romans 8:1 being one of them. We know that if we are in Christ, there is no condemnation. Why then, are so many Christians walking around with condemnation as their battle? Wrong thinking and patterns of disobedience could possibly be the short answer. It is one thing to know positional truths but quite another to know the God of the position. Certainly, that was my dilemma.

For decades, my reality was not in agreement with my theology. It resulted in much frustration. The Word of God states that "There's no condemnation to those in Christ." But the opposite was true in my life, not only was I swimming in it - I was drowning in it as well. My life didn't match the truth. This was something that I was not content to live with though I had become battle weary. I had a dogged determination that I would not leave this life without knowing true freedom and joy.

TEMPORARY RELIEF

We are only as healthy as our thought life. For decades, *healthy* would not have been used to describe my thought life. For a Jesus girl who loved Him and wanted to please Him with all my heart, there was a constant war within. Continual contention existed between what was and what was supposed to be—having my emotions as the barometer for how God felt about me on any given day

WE ARE ONLY AS HEALTHY AS OUR THOUGHT LIFE

was getting wearisome. They just weren't accurate. I think I paid too much attention to how I felt and the foreboding presence that seemed to be a constant companion. Feelings are not good indicators of where I'm truly at in life. They lie. They are fickle, and they can change with the weather. It certainly causes instability.

How we talk to ourselves about ourselves is very important. Knowing that my self-talk was damaging and destructive, I tried to find permanent relief in self-help books. I have read so many, and I did my best to apply the principles. For years I read scripture and prayed only to remain crippled with debilitating emotions. Those emotional bouts undermined all the hard work of mind renewal. There was a depth of frustration I could not describe.

The voice of the Holy Spirit and the voice of condemnation were vying for my ear. Any rejoicing from seeming breakthrough discoveries was quickly replaced with frustration when they did not last or were not sustainable. For whatever reason, my mind refused to believe what the Word of God said. I knew that the issue was me: the container, the vessel, the wineskin. Seeing all of the things God was pouring into my life just lying on the floor because my wineskin burst was getting tiring. I needed a new wineskin. Why couldn't I contain it?

A serious overhaul was in order; renewal in my mind plus deliverance and healing in my soul. That meant I had to go deeper— something beyond the intellect. Desperate enough to take the invitation to journey to deep, dark places of my soul with the Holy Spirit, I had to get out of my comfort zone. Even if it meant going against the flow and swimming upstream, I was determined to do it.

TAPPING INTO THE DIVINE

Pinpointing the source of my bondage was critical. I believed that I was unlovable. Believing that one is unlovable is typically a belief developed early in childhood due to many variables. That lie was sown early in the formative years of my life when my family was not yet born-again. I believe the enemy came to seed that early in my young, little soul for the harvest I would contend with later. Such deep-seated lies that were lodged within me had to be addressed before I could experience lasting freedom. Knowing that I had a responsibility to believe God's Word and doing life His way was the change I needed to make in my life.

> God is not a mortal like me, so I cannot argue with Him or take Him to trial. If only there were a mediator between us, someone who could bring us together. The mediator could make God stop beating me, and I would no longer live in terror of His punishment. Then I could speak to Him without fear, but I cannot do that in my own strength.
>
> JOB 9:32-35 NLT

Granted, Job's pain was attributed to his distorted thinking. But the intriguing thing to me is the cry for a mediator. That is who Jesus is and what He has done for us. The wrath of God was satisfied at Calvary's cross, and we need not live another day paying the fees to condemnation. There is no guilty stain of sin that Calvary's cross cannot reach. The price was paid, so we can go free without self-loathing. We are made righteous because of Jesus.

It is easy to think that God tolerates us at best. It is easier to believe that we have sinned too much and have gone too far for Him to help us. But nothing could be further from the truth. God loves us based on His nature, on who He is, and not on our own merit. I discovered that God is literally fond of us. Love is given and not earned. Though we don't deserve it, we can receive it. In a later chapter, I will discuss these truths in depth.

> GOD LOVES US BASED ON HIS NATURE, ON WHO HE IS, AND NOT ON OUR OWN MERIT

I believe that everything was provided for at the cross, but it was when I began to appropriate the truth of the cross to specific areas that I could exploit the breakthrough. Through this process, the cross became my friend. I learned how to live by dying. The Lord started to show me that I did not have to be stuck in the lowlands of condemnation. When condemnation threatens to overwhelm us, we have a choice. Like any other temptation, we must not yield to it. We can refuse the temptation to listen to the voice of defeat, failure, and fear. Do not be discouraged or disheartened, for there is a higher way to think.

> For as the heavens are higher than the earth, so are my ways higher than your ways and my thoughts than your thoughts.
>
> ISAIAH 55:9 ESV

God never said that we could not learn to think how He thinks. In fact, we not only can learn how, but we can know His thoughts. We have the mind of Christ and the Word of God to show us how to think according to the culture of the Kingdom.

> ## We have the mind of Christ.
> ### I CORINTHIANS 2:16 NIV

Having the mind of Christ means that we can access His thoughts, feelings, and attitudes and partake of His nature, enabling us to live and think differently. God-thoughts bring life.

Daily reframing our minds to live with a kingdom culture within takes effort. It requires some diligence, but I believe that God's grace empowers us to do what we cannot do in our own ability. You cannot think bad and live well. Having a right belief system will result in good behavior. I discovered that as Jesus brought inner healing to my damaged emotions and tormenting memories, my feelings began to line up. Right actions and behavior were the result.

Words matter. Words are containers carrying something. Sometimes it is best not to give voice to some of the thoughts running around in our heads. Some people have attributed this insightful saying to E.W. Kenyon who wisely stated, "Thoughts unspoken die unborn"! Whoever said it first must have been inspired by Jesus' words:

> ## For by your words, you will be justified, and by your words, you will be condemned.
> ### MATTHEW 12:37 NAS

The Proverb "As a man thinks in his heart so is he," is such a simple but profound truth. When we live out of emotion, we are easily swayed; however, when we live in truth we are free. We are not our emotions. Many times they will lie to us, but as we consistently go against how we feel, they eventually line up and become our ally. We must think about and speak about ourselves as God does. Then we can move from a place of abandonment to acceptance as we affirm the truth about ourselves. Truly when we invest the truth in ourselves, we can live in the truth.

The Spirit leads, demons drive. "Somebody teach me how to get them out of the driver's seat!" That was my cry. Understanding that I had an enemy, and there was an unseen battle for my mind, I had a responsibility to believe and act on the Word of God. I had to live it out. This scripture became more than just words to me.

> For though we walk in the flesh, we do not war according to the flesh. For the weapons of our warfare are not of the flesh, but mighty before God to the casting down of strongholds, casting down imaginations, and every high thing that is exalted against the knowledge of God, and bringing every thought into captivity to the obedience of Christ.
>
> 2 CORINTHIANS 10:3-5 ASV

What I came to realize in my journey was that if the enemy was going to be evicted, I had to grow strong enough to defeat it— some things you get delivered from, and other things you defeat. People can pray for you, encourage and support you, but at the end of the day, we must all face our demons and by the authority of Jesus drive them out and keep them out!

THE ROOT OF
THE MATTER

Though his height was like the height of cedars
and he was strong as the oaks; I even destroyed
his fruit above and his root below.

AMOS 2:9 NASB

It seemed like it was a million miles deep. But I had to take the brave journey to get to the root of the bad fruit in my life. This foul spirit was robbing my life of joy and freedom. Condemnation had done a number on me, and oftentimes the enemy would use my knowledge of scripture to beat me up rather than its intended purpose to build me up.

I felt as if God was always judging and finding fault with me, yet I knew from scripture that Jesus was already judged in my place. His Word stated that I am found in Him and above reproach. Still, there was this constant tension in which I lived of whether I was pleasing to God or not. This intense inner scrutiny became the lens from which I viewed life and other people. It became a kind of filter that distorted words and even sermons and made me defensive as if I was constantly being attacked.

But a major breakthrough came in a most unlikely place.

ROOTING FOR CHANGE

While flying across the country one autumn day, God began to minister to me from this portion of scripture. I had often viewed the scripture where Jesus talks about laying the axe to the root and fire purging us as a very scary indictment. Something changed inside me as I read it this time.

> Even now, God's axe of judgment is poised to chop down your barren tree right down to its roots! And every tree that does not produce good fruit will be leveled and thrown into the fire!
>
> LUKE 3:9 TPT

It dawned on me that God's axe was there to chop down something barren, something that was not producing in my life and holding back my potential. Let's face it! Condemnation was producing nothing good in or around me. It was limiting and stunting my growth. This wasn't an indictment but rather an observation. This was mercy. This was help. God had come not just to prune but to deal with those evil things at the very root. He judged those very things which were not producing good fruit in my life with the sword of His Word. He was cutting them down and throwing them in the fire, which speaks of complete annihilation. They cannot produce again if the root system is destroyed.

Clearly, Jesus wanted to lay the axe to the root. He goes to the source of the problem. Sadly, I was often busy trying to pick off the bad fruit. Ever trying to stop the negative self-talk, perfectionism, and driving attitudes, I failed to see that these were all outgrowths of a bad root system. That is until God showed up on that flight and took my blinders off. The axe goes to the root because God doesn't want it producing any more destruction. If there is something that is not producing good in my life, God will come and lay the axe to the root and burn it up in the fire.

I WAS BUSY TRYING TO PICK OFF THE BAD FRUIT, BUT GOD'S INTENTION WAS TO LAY THE AXE TO THE ROOT

I nearly jumped for joy, having never seen it this way before. My mind was trying to grasp this truth: *You mean I didn't have to cringe, hoping that God wouldn't notice the bad tree and fruit? You mean, I could see it from a different perspective? Like God's perspective, that gives hope and life?* The incredible discovery was a liberating revelation. God was not going to destroy me just because there was bad fruit in my emotions and thought life. The scripture that once brought torment was now adjusting my perspective. I began to see it from a different vantage point.

As the Holy Spirit began to align my mind with the Word properly, things were addressed. What a comfort it is to know that I can just rest in Him! As this truth became firmly established in my mind, the ungodly internal pressure to produce and perform began to lift off of me.

> I am the true grapevine, and My Father is the gardener. He cuts off every branch of Mine that doesn't produce fruit, and He prunes the branches that do bear fruit so they will produce even more.
> You have already been pruned and purified by the message I have given you. Remain in Me, and I will remain in you.

> For a branch cannot produce fruit if it is severed from
> the vine, and you cannot be fruitful unless you remain
> in Me. Yes, I am the vine; you are the branches.
>
> Those who remain in Me, and I in them, will produce
> much fruit. For apart from Me, you can do nothing.
>
> JOHN 15:1-5 NLT

The result was that I began to produce by virtue of my union with God. All I had to do was abide in Jesus. As I was abiding, good fruit was being produced in my life. It was slow but steady; it was almost effortless. This was way too easy in comparison to all the ungodly drive I had before with all the self-effort I exerted. This was the beginnings of what John referred to as abiding in Jesus at work in me. It's an amazing comfort to know that God is only removing from me what hinders me and what does not look like His Son. His method is so complete and swift that I need not suffer a moment longer. I only need to surrender.

THE TURNING

In coming to grips with this revelation, I had to repent for condemnation. I had to break my agreement with the lie of this culprit and stop empowering it. Up to that point, from studying scripture, I knew that it was wrong to dwell on the condemning thoughts. But I often battled the temptation to go with the condemnation because it felt comfortable and familiar. By God simply showing me that He's the One who has done the difficult and impossible part of the work, I can just rest. My internal striving can cease. That brought renewal in an area of lifelong deception.

Ending my habitual relationship with sin meant that I had to stop feeding my feelings. Too often, I think that we pay them too much attention. My own thoughts and emotions controlled me more than I cared to admit. What we do not feed, dies!

I had to learn to resist the devil on the onset and to become very aggressive about speaking the truth over my mind and arresting the thoughts—taking them captive. I had to stop agreeing with the devil. I had to deal with the passive posture of a victim, believing I had to endure its cruelty. It is sin to condemn yourself continually and agree with the accuser.

> So kill (deaden, deprive of power) the evil desire lurking
> in your members [those animal impulses and all that
> is earthly in you that is employed in sin]: sexual vice,
> impurity, sensual appetites, unholy desires, and all greed
> and covetousness, for that is idolatry (the deifying
> of self and other created things instead of God).
>
> COLOSSIANS 3:5 AMP

When truth began to penetrate my faulty belief system and dismantle the lies—something began to happen in my times with God. I began trusting that what I was hearing was true and that God just wanted me to come to Him when I sinned. I needed only to let Him bathe and make me clean again with His love and purifying blood. Something was changing. The fear began to lessen. In my pursuit to draw closer to God, in spite of the continual condemnation, I started experiencing life-changing and powerful encounters with Him. Though I had considered myself blessed before in all that I experienced with God, this was something new and thrilling. God was removing all that stood between us. Looking back on it, I know that as I kept drawing closer to God as James invited us to do, it was a deliberate act on my part.

> Draw near to God and He will draw near to you.
> Cleanse your hands, you sinners; and purify
> your hearts, you double-minded.

JAMES 4:8 NKJV

I cannot tell you how many times I have responded to God's invitation to come to Him. No words were uttered as I sat there a mess, feeling dirty and unloved. Remembering that He did say, "Come to me," I simply did. Over time, as my trust grew, I opened up to God the scary places, and He healed the deep places within me and began to change my desires. I removed the "No Trespassing" sign and let Him in on the hidden property of my inside world.

AS MY TRUST GREW, I OPENED UP TO GOD THE SCARY PLACES, AND HE HEALED THE DEEP PLACES WITHIN ME AND BEGAN TO CHANGE MY DESIRES

What about my nature that wanted to still run out and get dirty? I distinctly remembered the day that I prayed and got really honest with God. I told Him that I loved certain sins more than I loved Him. It was shameful, but I needed Him to help me to love Him more because I didn't. Also, I sinned because I chose to, and I stopped blaming everyone and everything (like my upbringing in a strict religious household included), and I took full responsibility for my choices. It was a brutally honest moment with God and a liberating one too.

How true it was when Dr. Michael Brown said in his book, *Hyper Grace*, "Repentance means spiritual revolution. Strongholds of sin are demolished. Lifetime bondages are overcome. Hardened hearts break open. Satan's grip is undone. Repentance sets the prisoner free." (pg. 88) I can testify that indeed this is what God has done in my life.

It begins with a really simple act. Confess your sin and forsake it. Break up with it. Ask God for forgiveness. It is in that moment that the blood of Jesus will wash away your sin and heal your wound. He came to bind up the brokenhearted. He loves you; every detail about you. If you will just fellowship with Jesus around the mess, He will tend to it. Run to Him, not from Him. Just show up and sit. This is a starting place.

The following is an excerpt from my journal about that particular experience:

Redeem the precious from the vile—

While hanging out with Jesus fellowshipping around His Word, He did what He so often does—speak to that place deep within, the place only He can touch and unlock. I admit that it always leaves me thirsty and longing for more of Him. I enter that place wanting many things, and I leave it only wanting one thing—more of God!

While reading in Luke 3 of John's message, the prophet of old was speaking to me, "... every twisted thing in your lives must be made straight! Every dark way must be brought to the light! Wrongs righted, injustices removed, every heart of pride will be humbled low before Him. Every deception will be exposed and replaced by the truth!" (TPT)

I had a decision to make—I could cruise right by the portion of scripture from the Passion Translation and merely peruse the writings and stimulate my intellect, or I could address the force I just felt hit my spirit.

Here? Right now? On this airplane soaring the heavens taking me across the country? Absolutely here! Right now!

I marveled at the willingness to go ahead and allow Holy Spirit to deal with me. But this year I made the decision I am not running from my Father anymore! He is willing to have the conversation, and I only need to be willing to go to that honest place.

I no longer care how vile are the things I need to discuss with Him, nor will I disguise them, but I will trust Him to still love me after I disclose them. I muster courage and go for it. So right there, on the jet, I talked with Jesus.

Viewing the portion of scripture again ... "Every twisted thing in your lives must be made straight! Every dark place must be brought to the light!"

"Well, here it is God, I invite you into this place of darkness once again. I have been having these damnable thoughts, desires, and enticements.

Your Word says it is twisted, wrong, and sinful. I agree with your Word! Save me, heal me, forgive me! These are not my thoughts. I will not go down this path, this line of thinking. It takes me from your presence Father, and I only want you! Save me from me. Please do not leave me to myself."

"Every deception will be exposed and replaced by the truth..." I choose truth just like Jesus did when He was tempted in the wilderness. I choose truth, and I bring these thoughts into the captivity of Jesus.

As I continued to read, the prophet John from the ancient writings spoke to me of Jesus ...

"He will baptize you into the spirit of Holiness and into His raging fire! He has in His hands the authority to judge your heart and the power to SIFT and CLEANSE you! He will separate the VALUABLE within you from that which is WORTHLESS. The valuable He will store up for use in His Kingdom, but He will burn the worthless in a fire no one can ever put out!"

He longs for my holiness, I long for my holiness, it is right there, available to me- I embrace it- the burning of your fire and Presence- your fire to burn deep inside of me and to purify me. All my desires, the longings of my soul—your heart is what I crave; your Presence is what I long to carry.

It had become my prayer ... Separate the valuable from the worthless. Redeem the precious from the vile. Sift and cleanse this heart from any part of it that wants something more than it wants You. May I never trade temporary, fleeting pleasure for Your Presence! May I never!

I am humbled by your love, Father God. I am no longer afraid of that love. I can sit in your Presence even here and bow before all you are and say that I am not afraid, nor am I condemned, but I am here with you asking you to continue this work, this glorifying, sanctifying work of consecration. Have all of me; let my surrender be that complete. My longing which satisfies. I need you; I long for you, I crave you. You are my desire, oh, beautiful one!

Permanent change happens on the inside first. This realization birthed a new desire in my life. Now I want what is growing in my life to please God, and if not, may I graciously yield to His process because it is only for my good and benefit. I can trust Him even when I don't understand. It reminded me of what Jesus told Peter, *"You don't understand now what I am doing, but someday you will"* *(John 13:7 NLT).*

5

GOD'S FATHER HEART

See how very much our Father loves us, for He
calls us His children, and that is what we are!

1 JOHN 3:1 NLT

I once preached a message titled, *"You wouldn't leave here and do a couple of lines of coke (cocaine), would you? Then don't do condemnation!"* To some people, condemnation is our vice. It is just as damaging as an illegal drug. Stewing in condemnation is illegal activity for a believer in the spirit realm. Yet, how many times was that my reality?

The truth is that we must turn from being inundated with condemnation because God gives us the grace to do so. If the Bible says there is no condemnation to those in Christ, then it is settled. In my case, I just needed the positional truth to become my experiential reality. I was determined to get it and to receive what was mine according to the Word. For me, one of those came in the form of a deep healing in my emotions and acceptance of the Father's continual, unconditional love and acceptance of me. It also included understanding His love and righteousness.

Evidence of the internal change was soon seen in my response to life. When I messed up and sinned, I would immediately confess, ask forgiveness and keep walking in close, intimate fellowship with the Father. This took cooperating with grace as I was accustomed to feeling horrible about the tiniest infraction and thought I had to beat myself up for days. Constantly, I had to remind myself that Jesus already took the beating. He was whipped so that I could be whole. In spite of my strong emotions contrary to grace, I wanted to honor His Word and work. I remember the day Jesus asked me to take the whip out of my hand. He knew that I knew about beating myself up. He knew my history.

RESCUED

It is not uncommon for teens to struggle with their identity as they are developing, but in my case, I literally hated myself. I thought that God could barely stand the sight of me because I was engaged in less than holy patterns of behavior. Under the pine tree was the beginning of many years of being sexually abused. That day had set in motion a magnetic force of dangerous deviants violating me. It was as if I had a neon sign on me that read, "Please molest me!" I did not feel like there was a safe place in my life. The gentle, loving Jesus in my child's mind was long gone. I loved Jesus but felt abandoned and unprotected by Him. Though I longed to be rescued out of the prison I was in, I felt hopeless that the pain could stop. It was a slow, painful death. The underlying unworthiness made a rescue seem impossible.

When I was fifteen years old, the self-hatred was so severe that I stood in front of a mirror and beat myself in the face. I gave myself a black eye. How I wished then that someone could have stopped me! Sadly, the driving voice demanding that I be punished for my guilt and wrongdoings was stronger than any care I had for myself. Despite my brokenness and self-loathing, I still wanted someone to love and rescue me.

Jesus knew that He needed to get the whip of condemnation out of my hand. But how? Without question, the only way He could do this for me – was with a God experience.

> The chastisement of our peace was upon Him;
> and with His stripes we are healed.
>
> ISAIAH 53:5 KJV

The revelation was vivid. Jesus' wounds from his trial, punishment, and death became so real to me that I was able to identify with them. I saw Jesus take upon Himself the anguish and torment that was resident in my mind, memory, and emotions. I saw Him being whipped so that I could be whole. Just as there were deeply entrenched strongholds in my thought life, there were deeply entrenched marks on His back from the whip. He bled so that I could be free from the crime of condemnation against me. Jesus died to destroy what was destroying me. How could my Savior love me like this?

Once again, I got a glimpse of the Jesus that I knew as a child. He hadn't left me after all! Just like He said, He would never leave me or forsake me (Hebrews 13:5). Though I had been carried away captive and thrown into a crypt of condemnation, my Savior had come to my rescue. He had thought me up and always knew this would be my journey. I had to bow at Calvary's cross and dump the condemnation I had been carrying for decades—how I fell in love with my Savior and loving Father once again!

Years later, on my second trip to Israel, our tour guide took us to a site called The Pit. It was where they held Jesus while awaiting trial. For all I knew about the Gospel story, for whatever reason, I did not realize this aspect. Our group descended down into a deep hole where, with every step, you felt more and more separated from the world above. We ended up in a small, completely enclosed opening known as The Pit. As our guide began to open scripture and share about the history of ancient punishments held in this solemn isolated enclosure where you can still feel the presence of condemnation and impending death, your mind travels back 2000 years, and you realize that this wasn't a tourist site in days past; it was a cold, dark, tormenting prison where people were placed to await their fate, often alone, with no food, just tormenting darkness and dread. They dropped Jesus into this pit, with walls of earth, darkness so black it would be unimaginable, a pit so deep escape was not a possibility. There He was condemned to wait for judgment.

While standing in that pit, weeping ensued; it is such a somber place of Jesus' horrendous suffering. I then had a vision; I saw Jesus being hoisted out of the pit with ropes underneath His arms, I saw His face wincing due to the rope burn as they were lifting Him out. I could not contain my emotion. He was lifted out of that pit to be condemned so I could go free? Something changed in me being so close to my Savior's suffering. What a sacrifice!

I thought of the words of Jesus in Matthew 12:11, "If one of you has a sheep and it falls into a pit"... Jesus had a little sheep stuck in a pit, and He took my place as my propitiation to go to the pit. My great substitute.

"Who redeems your life from the pit..."
PSALM 103:4

The questions Jesus asked Phillip in John 14 were now being asked to my heart. Whoever has seen me has seen the Father. How can you say, "Show us the Father?"

In that pit, in Israel, when I saw Jesus, I saw the Father.

A STANDING INVITATION

I believe God just wants to fellowship with us, even if it is around our weakness. A better way to say it is that God wants to hang out with us. I believe that He enjoys and wants our company. This was not something that I always believed. Sure, I had heard truths like this before, but I always felt that they were too good to be true. After some time, the truth began to pierce the armor of lies. Whatever we subject our souls to long enough, we become, whether the influence is a good or bad one.

WHATEVER WE SUBJECT OUR SOULS TO LONG ENOUGH, WE BECOME

As I mentioned before, I remember struggling with something that was defeating me on a consistent basis. It was a perpetual cycle of defeat and failure. Regardless of how I tried, I seemed to be rendered helpless in breaking the cycle. Frustrated by all my futile attempts, efforts, and "do-better" philosophies, I decided to try what has been a standing invitation in God's Word.

> "Then Jesus said, 'Come to Me, all of you who are weary and carry heavy burdens, and I will give you rest.'"
>
> MATTHEW 11:28 NLT

So I figured, why not just go to God—broken, imperfect, with my performance at an all-time low? Why not humble myself and present God with the reality of who I am rather than the idealistic version of who I thought I should be? After all, that person did not exist.

With emotions warring against my decision to be brutally honest with God, I drew close to Him and said, "God, here I am. I'm in pain. I'm constantly failing. I hurt, and I'm miserable. Can you heal me? Will you help me? How do I change? How do I heal? I cannot see what is in my way! How do I become free? I am just going to show up. I'm just going to hang out with You." That was the beginning.

So I began to show up regardless of my contrary emotions and thoughts that screamed I was "too this or too that," and I kept falling on the mercies of God. I would come a mess and leave feeling better—more stable, peaceful, and with a greater understanding of His love. God would simply love on me, speak to my heart, heal, and deliver areas of my life that needed healing. His peace would both cover and comfort me. Little by little, I began to feel more secure.

WHERE I BELONG

And The Lord said, "Behold, there is a place by
me, and thou shalt stand upon the rock."

EXODUS 33:21 KJV

The principle in this scripture became the one that I took hold of during that process. Discovering that I had a place with God was mind-blowing. Yes, even a place that was right beside Him! I had waited my entire life for this. Finally, I found where I belonged.

What I grasped was this truth: God the Father, the Son, and the Holy Spirit desired communion with me. The Godhead wanted to fellowship with me, or as I would say, *"hang out"* with me. It spoke to me of identity and who I really was, a born-again daughter of God. I belonged; I was not an orphan but a daughter. Not only was I a daughter of God, but also I was celebrated. This was like contraband. Questions began to flood me: *You mean I didn't have to perform for all this? There is actually hope? My perfectionism and obsession with all the mistakes and mishaps could be traded? There is a great exchange available? Could I give Jesus all I am and receive all He is?* The answers to all these were a resounding, "Yes!"

Small differences were beginning to show up in me. I couldn't wait to get back to His presence. He was coming. He was just there. New thoughts entered my mind, such as *God is fond of you. He enjoys His time with you. God looks forward to it. He has something on His heart to share with you.* Understand this when I say that these thoughts breaking in were radical. These were thoughts that I was not accustomed to permeating my mind. It was like rays of sunshine after a lifetime of cloudy, dreary days.

Understanding was dawning on me concerning God's love for me. Jesus has mercy for our failures and those of others. He is not a scorekeeper demanding perfection. He is not insecure, and He longs to heal our insecurity and identity so we can enjoy fellowship with Him regardless of the root cause. After all, He died to make peace between our Father and us.

A depiction of the Father's love for us when we sin is demonstrated beautifully in the story of the Prodigal son (Luke 15). Upon His return from a rebellious, sinful condition, his father received him with love that celebrated him. Like the prodigal, we can find that the Father's arms are always open to welcome us home where we belong. No matter why we left home, He is always happy to see us come back.

TUNED TO HIS VOICE

Undoubtedly, I was used to gavels and rulers measuring my performance and value. These forms of judgment and measuring were more discouraging than not. Obviously, I never measured up, and so I judged that I was not good enough. Without fail, this line of thinking always finds you wanting as you will come up short, less than, and second rate. Metrics as these only leave one marginalized!

We have thoughts running around in our heads that are not in God's heart. Trying to please God by trying harder is not even doable. You're His child. He is pleased. Your person has nothing to do with your performance. However, I will say that the Father is pleased when we are obedient to Him just as we are pleased with our own children. It is quite clear in scripture that there is blessing on obedience. God's love for us is based on His nature; He is love. It is who He is. It is what He does, and He just loves us. Love is who He is. Love is given not earned. We cannot earn it; however, we can learn to receive it.

The Father speaks to us in gentle, kind tones and, at times, if necessary, in fatherly, firm tones. In fact, if He disciplines us, it is because He loves us, and this proves that we are His children. As a Father, God addresses sin. His holy nature demands it, and He despises what sin does to His children. The Holy Spirit will convict us of sin and convince us to turn to the Father and receive His forgiveness, cleansing, and love as He desires no disruption in our fellowship. Sin is a great disrupter. God does not speak to us in accusing, angry and harsh tones. Oftentimes the voices we hear are people from childhood—an angry father or a demanding mother. But Father God's voice sounds like none of those. He is not man.

Statistics show there is a large portion of society that cannot relate to the reality of a father due to having no father in the home. This has caused an increase in an orphan spirit resulting in an independent spirit. Others who had fathers in the home who were emotionally distant or portrayed an inaccurate, abusive, or domineering style of parenting also struggle in their perception and understanding of the heavenly Father. Regardless of where we come from, God desires to reveal His heart and be a Father over us.

It is damaging if our earthly father and mother could not effectively model the perfect parent of Father God, but perhaps they did the best they could with what they knew. I refuse to condemn or blame my parents or anyone else for anything when I have the perfect parent available to me—Father God. He can now make the crooked places straight and take the wrongs and make them right. He can re-parent any of us.

Blaming previous generations is counterproductive. Forgive and live rather than shame and blame. I do believe in dealing with generational curses and appropriating the cross of Christ; however, I refuse to be stuck because someone before me dropped me. I think of Jonathan's son Mephibosheth (2 Samuel) when word came of a kingdom change, his nurse grabbed him in haste and fell and crippled him. She didn't mean to, but in her attempt to rescue him, she maimed him. Perhaps our parents or caretakers did the best they could with the condition their soul was in at the time? Perhaps if I had to face what they did, I might not have fared any

FORGIVE AND LIVE IS BETTER THAN SHAME AND BLAME

better. It is best for me, for all of us, to stay above the fray and not get into the blame game. Forgiveness is the way to stay in the no-condemnation zone. I encourage you to forgive the person(s) who dropped you. They cannot give to you what you seek. They cannot pay you back. Only Jesus can bring restoration.

AUTHOR'S NOTE CONCERNING THE PIT:

We know from history that Jesus was tried and spent the night at the House of Caiaphas.[1] The Old Testament points out multiple times that the pit was a form of punishment.[2]

ENDNOTES

1. Cross reference the end of Matthew 26 to the beginning of Matthew 27, and the end of Mark 14 to the beginning of Mark 15.
2. Cross reference Isaiah 24:22, ESV. "They will be gathered together as prisoners in a pit, they will be shut up in prison, and after many days they will be punished."

6

FACED WITH GRACE

And Jesus said, "I do not condemn you,
either. Go. From now on sin no more."

JOHN 8:11 NAS

A quiet getaway to the wintery, sleepy southern shore town was my plan. Instead, I spent the evening listening to the harrowing confessions of a woman trapped in a cycle of sexual immorality. This was not what I had in mind. After all, my trip was not just to escape the winter snowstorm that was pummeling the east coast, but also to write. However, this is the life I live as a minister. When someone finally musters the courage to come clean, you help him or her to unload the burden. It was interesting how she kept referring to condemnation over and over.

She began to let out her secrets like the burst of a dam. It was plain to see that she was experiencing freedom with every admission. Yet she was conflicted. She went from confession to condemnation and then back again. It was like a merry go round. Shame, secrecy, and lies had her silenced. For nearly a year and a half, she admitted that she had wanted to take me into her confidence but felt too condemned. Immediately I thought, *Ah, yes! The condemnation crypt that haunts!* I was familiar with it. How it holds you in its grip away from truth, freedom, and light!

Thankfully, grace broke through, and she found some freedom, but it certainly got me to thinking. Remember the woman caught in the act of adultery in Jesus' time? In the very act! I have often wondered if the Pharisees and the Scribes immediately dragged her out in the street by the hair of her head. Or did they at least allow her to grab a cloak to cover herself as they were about to strip her of any remaining thread of dignity before the crowd outside? Also, if she was caught in the very act, what happened to the man who was caught along with her? I have a feeling that they let their buddy leave out the back door before the drama unfolded. After all, the Mosaic Law demanded that he be stoned as well (Deuteronomy 22:22).

Obviously, they were merely using this woman's sin to further their cause. They weren't really concerned about morality and holiness but in using the situation as a means to trap and accuse Jesus. They hated Him and knew that they had Him dead to rights. In their minds, He would have to enforce the Law of Moses or risk losing credibility with the crowd and the momentum of His ministry.

ENCOUNTERING MERCY

Once again, they underestimated Jesus. Initially, He almost ignored them as they paraded the woman in the street and stopped at Him. I can hear the tone of their sanctimonious voices, "This woman was caught in the act of adultery, in the very act. Moses said we should stone her. What do you say?" They waited with smug arrogance.

This they said to test Him, hoping they might find a charge against Him.

What would Jesus say now? What could He say? He had outsmarted them to this point, but finally, they had Jesus! They would watch the son of man squirm. Instead, He ignored them. The deafening silence grew past awkward while Jesus was just there, silent. After all, what they were saying was true. She did sin. She was trapped in immorality, caught by its enticement and lure. Much like the dear soul, I was listening to that day.

Jesus ignored the accusations. He stooped down and wrote on the ground with his finger. That reminded me of Paul's revelation.

> He (Jesus) ever lives to make intercession for us.
>
> HEBREWS 7:25 KJV

It was only after the accusers persisted that He raised Himself up and finally spoke, "He who is without sin, cast the first stone." That was not the answer they expected to get, nor the permission they needed to carry out her sentence. So nothing happened. They didn't throw a single rock.

Jesus bent down again and continued to write in the sand. It has been speculated what He wrote, yet scripture leaves it to our imaginations. The one thing we do know is that Jesus' reply pricked their hearts, and one by one, from the eldest to the youngest, they left convicted. Jesus was left alone with the woman standing there before Him, in the center of the court. Read the resulting conversation:

> When Jesus raised Himself up, He said to her, "Woman where are your accusers? Has no man condemned you?"

She answered, "No one Lord!"
And Jesus said, "I do not condemn you either. Go
on your way and from now on sin no more."

JOHN 8:10-11 AMP

Imagine when she finally mustered the courage to look up and see no one standing around her. It must have been total and complete shock. I can only imagine the emotional roller coaster this woman experienced. She went from being with her lover to being intruded upon and then grabbed by a murderous mob moments before being publicly shamed. Scared senseless, she knew her fate and was anticipating the stoning. I know I would have been. The whole event was, however, interrupted by mercy. She encountered a man who offered redemption rather than retribution. He gave her mercy instead of judgment, conviction rather than condemnation.

JESUS OFFERED HER REDEMPTION RATHER THAN RETRIBUTION, MERCY INSTEAD OF JUDGMENT, CONVICTION RATHER THAN CONDEMNATION

Jesus told her, "Neither do I condemn you, go and sin no more." How profound! How scandalous! He was essentially saying, "I'm not mad at you. I am not judging you or sentencing you to death. But go and sin no more. I will now provide you with the grace to live a different life. I will show you a better way, a more excellent way to live."

SPIRIT OF GRACE

I believe one by one, the things that contribute to the condemnation of our life are often dealt with by the spirit of grace. This was certainly true in my journey as the lies that I had believed were uprooted. These falsehoods had contributed to my messed up belief system.

Michael Brown, Ph.D., said in his book, *Go and Sin No More,* "If you are a born-again believer, a blood-washed child of God, you are not damned and doomed. God is not saying, 'To hell with you! Depart from me, you wicked one.' Absolutely not! He is saying, 'You are Mine! I accept you fully through my Son.' What then is the difference between conviction and condemnation? Conviction says to the believer, 'You have sinned, so come to Me!' Condemnation says to the damned sinner, 'You are pronounced guilty. Away from Me!'"

Mercy triumphs over judgment. We cannot attack areas of weakness in our lives. Truth without grace is brutal. With Jesus came grace and truth. He gives us the grace to live the truth. When I learned to accept and forgive the unacceptable and despised parts of myself, grace entered through new avenues. I embraced the fact that, at that point, Christ died for me. He didn't die for me when things were perfect and going well. He died for all the fall-out that I would experience as a result of sin. He died for my sin-sick, bankrupt soul. He died so that I could have peace with Father God and enjoy His presence. His blood ransomed me, and I cannot let something as cheap as condemnation destroy me or my walk.

What would your life look like if lived in an atmosphere of grace? It is an intriguing question. We must take our lead from the Father. He loved and approved of Jesus before He ever did anything. After Jesus' baptism and before His public ministry began, we have the Father expressing His heart toward His Son.

> And behold, a voice out of the heavens said, "This is
> My beloved Son, in whom I am well-pleased."
>
> MATTHEW 3:17 NAS

The same merciful Jesus that the nameless woman of the Bible encountered is still at work today, not condemning but redeeming those trapped in cycles of sin. Our repentance opens the floodgates of forgiveness and safeguards us against condemnation that would isolate us in fear. We are not meant to live separate from God's fellowship but to have unbroken fellowship with Him. We only need to break our relationship to sin, as it always pays in destruction.

RUNNING INTO HOPE

I recall another life-changing shift while sitting in my prayer chair and telling God, "I can sit here and go over all my short-comings, or I can sit here in gratitude and worship You. I can focus on myself, or I can lift my eyes and focus on You and trust that You are bigger than me and all my issues."

Again, something changed inside me that day. I learned that He loved me so much that He would fellowship with me around my weakness, and each time I left His Presence, I was stronger. Permanent change was happening from the inside out.

These verses became keys for me in walking out of sin-cycles.

> For by the death He died, He died to sin [ending His relation to it] once for all; and the life that He lives, He is living to God [in unbroken fellowship with Him]. Even so consider yourselves also dead to sin and your relation to it broken, but alive to God [living in unbroken fellowship with Him] in Christ Jesus.

Let not sin therefore rule as king in your mortal (short-
lived, perishable) bodies, to make you yield to its cravings
and be subject to its lusts and evil passions. Do not
continue offering or yielding your bodily members [and
faculties] to sin as instruments (tools) of wickedness.
But offer and yield yourselves to God as though you
have been raised from the dead to [perpetual] life,
and your bodily members [and faculties] to God,
presenting them as implements of righteousness.

For sin shall not [any longer] exert dominion over you,
since now you are not under Law [as slaves], but under
grace [as subjects of God's favor and mercy].

ROMANS 6:10-14 AMP

Living a life with freedom and a new understanding of God's grace is evident in so many areas of my life. Peace is permeating my person and dismantling the lies of performance and perfectionism. I do not have to perform or make the grade to be loved. It is something that I had to learn to get used to, and to a degree, I still am.

I love the words of D.L. Moody

"Christ died for sin;
The believer dies to sin;
The unbeliever dies in sin."

Whenever sin is around, something is dying somewhere. Whenever there's an understanding of God's grace, someone is awakening to real life.

LIKE THE SCRIBES AND PHARISEES,
WE ALSO UNDERESTIMATE JESUS.
WE EXPECT HIS RETRIBUTION, WE ARE
SURPRISED TO ENCOUNTER HIS GRACE.

JESUS GIVES US THE GRACE TO LIVE IN
TRUTH—FREE FROM SIN, FREE FROM SHAME,
FREE FROM CONDEMNATION. AMEN!

7

COVERED BY LOVE

Such love has no fear, because perfect love expels all fear.
If we are afraid, it is for fear of punishment, and this shows
that we have not fully experienced His perfect love.
We love each other because He loved us first.

1 JOHN 4:18, 19 NLT

ove God, love people is a popular saying inspired by scripture, but it is impossible to love others if we do not love ourselves. Nor is it possible if we have not learned to receive the love that has been bestowed on us by the Father through the Son. Jesus himself said, "Love your neighbor as yourself." That's it. We must have a healthy love of ourselves. I'm not talking about being a narcissist. Rather it is a true love that honors ourselves as God's handiwork.

We know that as Christians, we are to live and walk in love, and yet there has been much criticism that we do not. Is it that perhaps we need to live and walk in the Father's love towards ourselves? We cannot give away what we do not have. At best, our love will be superficial. None of us can live outside of our character, so if we really are shallow in love, it will show up in our relationships. How we love people really is an indicator of our love walk towards ourselves. Walking in love is a must. As the saying goes, "A step out of love is a step into sin."

Consider the manner of love that God has poured out on us. He does not nit-pick, find fault, or criticize us. He does not look at us and wag His head in shame, disappointment, and disapproval. He does not loathe us or our presence. These are all lies! Identify them as such. Who would fellowship with a God like that? Sadly that is the distorted image of God many have and why they avoid Him. They do not know who He is or what He is really like. What kind of God do we serve?

NO FEAR IN LOVE

God is love. He is not the concept of love. He is love. That is who He is, and it is what He does. It is His nature. God's perfect love casts out fear. This includes fear's cousins—panic and anxiety. His love dispels fear because it cannot stand in His presence. That means every fear, including the fear of rejection and not being perfect.

> Such love has no fear, because perfect love expels all fear. If we are afraid, it is for fear of punishment, and this shows that we have not fully experienced His perfect love. We love each other because He loved us first.
>
> 1 JOHN 4:18, 19 NLT

Whatever hang-ups you may have concerning sin that keep you from God, know that He sent Jesus to deal with the sin issue. He is a Holy God. Sin had to be punished. That is why Jesus took our place of punishment and became our substitute not because He had to, but because He chose to. God wanted to ransom and restore us. He did this because of His great love. It was all His idea. He thought up the redemption plan. No price was too high for Him to pay. Jesus sacrificed Himself willingly with the very hope that we would come to God the Father. There was no guarantee that we would come, yet He still laid His life down with the very hope that we would respond to His love.

> "O God, hear my prayer. Listen to my heart's cry.
> For no matter where I am, even when I'm far from
> home, I will cry out to You for a Father's help."
>
> PSALM 61:1-2 TPT

Realize that the less than ideal parts of us are only healed through exposing them to the Father's unconditional love. He accepts us in spite of them. The only way that I can feel good about myself is to receive God's unconditional love into every place of me, and nothing is off-limits or hands-off. Every dark, scary crevice in my soul must be exposed to His light, love, and truth. It often requires my courage and willingness to go there with God. He respects my "no," but that keeps me stuck in the lowlands. Light shines in the dark and expels the operations in the shadows.

> Such hope never disappoints or deludes or shames
> us, for God's love has been poured out in our hearts
> through the Holy Spirit Who has been given to us.
>
> ROMANS 5:5 AMP

The enemy of condemnation wants us to withdraw from love. That is the only way it can gain an entry point and do its evil work.

SELF-ACCEPTANCE

It is commendable to desire an ideal thing, but we must live in the reality of what is. Reality locates us. We must divorce the lie of idealism. The ideal perfect version of ourselves is a fictitious fantasy that can cause us to chase an illusion. The legend in our minds is not even attainable. Of course, the enemy keeps us busy and exhausted, running on the treadmill of the ideal self. Yet there is no ideal self. There is only the real, raw, but authentic self. It is possible to live and accept ourselves in the reality of who we are without condemnation. And that person is loved and accepted fully in Christ. Yes, that person is expected to grow and change and attain to Christ-likeness in character.

> THERE IS NO IDEAL SELF—ONLY THE REAL, RAW, AUTHENTIC SELF EXISTS, AND THIS IS THE SELF WE MUST LEARN TO ACCEPT

Jesus said to the disciples, "Come follow me, and I will make you fishers of men" (Matthew 4:19). The words, "I will make you," imply we are becoming—we are in the process of becoming something we currently are not. There is a big difference between becoming and performing. One implies room for growth; the other does not. We are being made into His image; we are not performing to get His image. In this process, we are celebrated and cheered. The journey is the destination.

Accept yourself, even your weaknesses, imperfections, and areas where you are immature. Rather than presiding as the judge and constantly passing sentences to condemn, we would far better serve ourselves in embracing those less desirable areas and looking to Jesus, our advocate, for defense and help. You are not your struggle, so don't let it define you.

When we accept ourselves, we can then freely confess wrongs without believing that our being is wrong. God accepts you! He called us, knowing what we were. He knows things about us that we have yet to discover. Some of those are not so pleasant. When we do come face to face with our imperfections, His love is present—awaiting us as His grace enables us to walk through the pain of self-discovery.

We are to love unconditionally and accept ourselves, as God loves us. After all, we were fearfully and wonderfully made in His image, each one of us thought up in the heart of our Father and created by Jesus. With that in mind, we should also consider how we speak to His creation. Would you speak to your neighbor the way you speak to yourself? Dishonoring tones towards self are also not acceptable. Could you imagine Jesus riding, judging, and condemning us? Some of us raised in legalistic homes certainly can because that is what we were taught to believe and come to expect. But I assure you, that is not the voice of Jesus. I learned to distinguish the voice of a stranger from that of the Shepherd (John 10:4-5).

Again, I'm not speaking of narcissistic self-love but rather receiving unconditional love and a sense of righteousness through Jesus that silences the voice of condemnation. An overly sensitive and critical conscience needs only to experience total acceptance. It is in experiencing the truths of scripture we confess that results in change.

AN OVERLY SENSITIVE AND CRITICAL CONSCIENCE
NEEDS ONLY TO EXPERIENCE TOTAL ACCEPTANCE TO
EMBRACE THE TRUTHS OF SCRIPTURE AND SEE CHANGE

EXTENDING KINDNESS

Grace and truth liberate us. We must deal with the truth and reality of who we are with some toleration. Accept not reject. Be kind rather than be harsh and angry. It is time to trade in the abusive, demanding self and allow a gentler, kinder version of self to emerge. The Holy Spirit is present to help us transform to this end. Personally, the harsh self-talk had to be replaced with a kinder, gentler tone and attitude. Below are two portions of my scriptural arsenal that I used to develop this tone and attitude toward myself.

> Instead, be kind to each other, tenderhearted, forgiving one another, just as God through Christ has forgiven you.
>
> EPHESIANS 4:32 NLT

Yes, this refers to our treatment of others, but how different would our lives look if we applied this scriptural attitude and tone towards ourselves?

> Since God chose you to be the holy people He loves, you must clothe yourselves with tenderhearted mercy, kindness, humility, gentleness, and patience.
>
> Make allowance for each other's faults, and forgive anyone who offends you. Remember, the Lord forgave you, so you must forgive others.
>
> Above all, clothe yourselves with love, which binds us all together in perfect harmony. And let the peace that comes from Christ rule in your hearts.
>
> COLOSSIANS 3:12-15 NLT

There are some things that we must shut our minds against and refuse to do. Make the choice to be kind. How many of us have heard as a child, "If you have nothing nice to say, say nothing at all." Unedifying and destructive inner self-derision is one of those habits that need to go. Is adopting a compassionate approach to ourselves really that ridiculous? Sadly for many years, I thought that it was. I thought it was awkward to be kind to myself. Now I think that if I could be courteous to a stranger, then why not to myself?

Ironically, it was people loving and accepting me that helped paved the way for my own acceptance of mercy.

Honoring yourself is honoring God's handiwork. Think about it. He created us as a masterpiece, and yet we nit-pick, criticize, and scrutinize it. I thought in patterns like this for so long; I thought it was normal. It wasn't until my self-talk was overheard that someone called me out on it. They said, "Hey, do not talk to my friend that way!" I was floored; I could tell they meant it.

We must not only love and accept ourselves but others as well. How can we give away what we don't possess? How will we accept others if we have difficulty accepting ourselves? How can we love our neighbor if we do not love ourselves?

Condemnation isolates us. The cure is found being insulated in His presence and in life-giving relationships with others. There were times I was just done; I could not pretend another moment. I would isolate, I would go to my hiding place and berate myself rather than reach to another. I felt unworthy of reaching out to God or people.

As I update this manuscript, "social-distancing" is the new normal as we are fighting the invisible, microscopic enemy of COVID 19. The sacrifice the country is making in an attempt to save lives is also having a side effect. There is a rise in depression in some due to the lack of interaction. Humans are relational; we are not meant to live isolated. God said of Adam, "It's not good for man to dwell alone..."

Often, the kindness I found in those dark days was through another extending to me grace and acceptance when I felt unworthy. They came after me in my isolation and modeled love and acceptance. Their kindness gave hope. If another person could be compassionate to me, if they could love me, was it not because they loved themselves? The model I saw was their love for God enabled them to love themselves and their neighbor. I was on to something—others loving me long before I ever started loving and accepting myself. Acceptance is the answer to that dilemma because acceptance is grace. That means accepting the bad parts or the less than ideal parts of me. We have to learn to develop a loving and kind tone towards ourselves. Put simply, this was a matter of love breaking through the fog of condemnation.

Generally, relationships suffer due to feeling unworthy as we tend to resist love and acceptance and instead try to convince others that we are bad and not worth loving. Self-destruction and rejection are hard taskmasters. If we exceed another's limitation, we are left isolated and alone, furthering the condemnation cycle as we tell ourselves, "I'm too much for people to love." Such tendencies need to be confronted and resisted. When others can accept and understand our frailties and weaknesses (in my case, it was my husband and some choice friends), we can learn to accept them as part of our real self, versus some ideal version that does not exist. I can learn not to see myself as the

SELF-DESTRUCTION AND REJECTION ARE HARD TASKMASTERS

grandiose, ideal person I would like to be. I can learn to accept and forgive myself despite my limitations and shortcomings and lean into the grace of God, which is His enabling ability to do what I cannot do.

FREEDOM IN LOVE

Consistently tell yourself the truth. Move from a fear and punishment reality to one of love and acceptance. Refuse to have a harsh and judgmental view of yourself. Quickly forgive yourself for failures, confess them, and move forward. Stop beating yourself up over failures and mistakes. This was so severe in my life. Having internalized the thought of consistently being a failure, I literally punished myself with a beating resulting in a black eye. Sure, that was pretty extreme, but a deeply rooted and domineering voice of condemnation can cause you to do extreme things to satisfy it. That voice has an appetite. It is a frightening thing when we are both judge and jury and have the power to carry out the indictment. I doubt that many will stand in front of a mirror and engage in self-deprecating behavior, but isn't that what you're doing internally? You're beating yourself up for failures, weaknesses, imperfections, and mistakes.

The solution is a matter of repentance. Yes, godly sorrow leads to repentance. That is God's way. There is no need to judge and condemn ourselves any longer. That is an ineffective way to deal with it, and it does not work. Remember, Jesus paid the price for our sin. Ask for forgiveness, embrace it, and then keep moving.

I am learning to stand boldly in grace, where judgment and condemnation are not invited.

Therefore, since we have been made right in God's sight
by faith, we have peace with God because of what Jesus
Christ our Lord has done for us. Because of our faith,
Christ has brought us into this place of undeserved
privilege where we now stand, and we confidently
and joyfully look forward to sharing God's glory.

ROMANS 5:1 NLT

When we struggle with sin cycles and behavioral problems resulting in lapses, the condemnation starts, then we return to the very behaviors we were trying to leave in an effort to find relief from the terrible feelings we're experiencing. You can see the trap.

Condemnation hinders, love heals. All any of us desire is love and acceptance, and many of us have searched for it in all the wrong places. Plenty of my choices left me even more broken and damaged than I already was. I'm not even sure I would have recognized what it was for which I was looking. His mercy found me. He not only demonstrated it in His Son but through some of His choice children.

My focus and aim is God's love. I'm on a quest for it. It is my prayer that my walk with God would be so attractive to others that they would want to know Him and His presence. I pray my love for Him provokes a longing for the same loving relationship in others.

8

RENEWING THE MIND

And that you be renewed in the spirit of your mind, and
put on the new self, which in the likeness of God has been
created in righteousness and holiness of the truth.

EPHESIANS 4:23-24 NAS

Awakened at 3:30 am, I heard a certain tone in my head. This was during a particular battle with condemnation, where I was weary because strong emotions and tormenting thoughts battered my mind. Now, I don't always discern right away that these thoughts aren't necessarily mine. The tone was definitely disapproving and unkind. Immediately, I heard the Father's whisper in my heart challenge it, "That is not my voice!" Instantly, to my great relief, the change came, and I was able to tune into the loving nature of My heavenly Father. I had distinguished the difference with that whisper. Here's what I heard my Father say and what I later penned in my journal.

Is that my voice or yours? Do I feel that way about
you? NO! It is not my voice; rather it is yours.
I do not feel that way about you! My thoughts

are good, of compassion and mercy, of loving-kindness and faithfulness. My sheep know my voice. The voice of another, they do not follow. Break agreement with that voice, your voice. Fire the Judge! Fire yourself!"

My mind knew how to think in old thought patterns of defeat, failure, fear, and insecurity. It was automatic, like a default button. So familiar. But it didn't have to remain that way. I simply had to stop tolerating it. Discovering that it is possible to think differently gave me an anchor of hope. Freedom was drawing near. During my times with Jesus, I realized that I wasn't in this struggle alone. The thing about freedom is, it isn't free, and it requires work. Apparently, if I was willing to trade my time to renew my mind on a consistent daily basis, then transformation was bound to happen. It was only a matter of time. God is faithful to complete the good work that He began in me.

> For I am confident of this very thing, that He who began a good work in you will perfect it until the day of Christ Jesus.
>
> PHILIPPIANS 1:6 NASB

We were made in His image. Our desire to soar comes from that image. Consequently, sin broke us and resulted in our tendency to sink into our weaknesses. God wants to restore us so that our thoughts are in line with His thoughts about us. We cannot go on to live victorious, productive lives with negative, faulty thought systems running through our brains. It is only a matter of time before our inside world shows up, and what was evident only to you and quite possibly a few others, could become evident to more people depending on your sphere of influence. Whether you're influencing a child or adult, leading one or many people, to live in conflict is tormenting and will spill over in various toxic ways. We can only hide and pretend for so long. Eventually, what we are shows up.

WALKING IT OUT

I am radical about mind renewal. Seeing the transformation in my own life and in the lives of others has been inspirational, to say the least. Thinking like Jesus is a necessity for an abundant and victorious life. My heart's cry to Father God is *I delight to do Your will*. The love of God had to heal the places in my heart where the lies lodged. Habitually, I began to do things like constantly affirming the truth of scripture and what God said about my identity and me. These were some of the truths I had to tell myself in place of the lies:

> God values me.
> I am loved and accepted.
> I am His handiwork.
> I am forgiven, loved, and healed.

I wasn't just saying these truths; I was meditating upon them, day and night, and intentionally making them a part of my inner constitution. By His grace, I was rewriting it with a pen of mercy. This was a conscious effort to believe what God, my Creator, said about me rather than what the devil, the liar, said. Changing what I chose to believe, say, and think enabled my emotions to line up accordingly, producing right actions and responses to life. This did take some time. I had no unrealistic expectations of overnight success. I was years deep in this pitiful pit; however, I was determined to be faithful to win the day. I heard a preacher say one time, "Faithfulness is long obedience in the same direction." That was my goal. Win every day by being faithful.

My emotions were resistant to my confession for years. Somehow I found the courage to stay in there and kept seeding my mind with truth. Often I wondered if they were ever going to take root. I was tempted to quit and did many times, only to feel condemned for being a quitter—thus, the cycle would perpetuate. Drilling my mind with truth was, at times, tedious and tiresome, yet neglecting to do so resulted in a not so desirous outcome. I decided then that I would rather do the work to think clearly than the work to climb out of pits I could slide into through passivity. I also began to speak the truth with which I was seeding my mind. I would say it out of my mouth despite the mob of mocking I heard in my mind. I was operating on a faith principle. I was calling those things that were not as though they were (Romans 4:17).

> I COULD EITHER DO THE WORK TO THINK CLEARLY, OR WORK TO CLIMB OUT OF PITS I SLID INTO THROUGH PASSIVITY—IT WAS GOING TO BE WORK EITHER WAY

Unruly thoughts that were antagonistic to the truth of the Lord Jesus concerning me had to be crucified. Also, I had to be in agreement with God and call myself crucified. After reading the portion of scripture below, I concluded that if this principle were the key to living an overcoming life, then surely the same thing would apply to condemnation. Taking these verses, I would walk the floor and agree with what the Word said about the war in my mind and emotions.

If then, you have been raised with Christ [to a new life,
thus sharing His resurrection from the dead], aim at
and seek the [rich, eternal treasures] that are above,
where Christ is, seated at the right hand of God.

And set your minds and keep them set on what is above (the
higher things), not on the things that are on the earth.

COLOSSIANS 3:1-2 AMP

God's thoughts are higher, better, and purer than my thoughts.
He cannot think a bad thought.

For [as far as this world is concerned] you have died,
and your [new, real] life is hidden with Christ in God.
When Christ, Who is our life, appears, then you also
will appear with Him in [the splendor of His] glory.

So kill (deaden, deprive of power) the evil desire lurking
in your members [those animal impulses and all that
is earthly in you that is employed in sin]: sexual vice,
impurity, sensual appetites, unholy desires, and all greed
and covetousness, for that is idolatry (the deifying
of self and other created things instead of God).

It is on account of these [very sins] that the [holy] anger
of God is ever coming upon the sons of disobedience
(those who are obstinately opposed to the divine
will), among whom you also once walked, when you
were living in and addicted to [such practices].

COLOSSIANS 3:3-7 AMP

This truth is one to keep before me always. Once I thought and
lived this way, but with God's power, I do not have to be this way
anymore. This portion of scripture implies choice. I am free to
choose.

But now put away and rid yourselves [completely] of all these things: anger, rage, bad feeling toward others, curses and slander, and foulmouthed abuse and shameful utterances from your lips! Do not lie to one another, for you have stripped off the old (unregenerate) self with its evil practices.

COLOSSIANS 3:8, 9 AMP

I am now able to be an expression of God's heart toward others.

You have heard the saying, *"How do you eat an elephant?* The answer is, of course, *"One bite at a time."* This was my elephant. I just kept eating it. It took time and effort. I fought discouragement, but there is something about just staying in there until it eventually turns. It is about being consistent. We change when we daily do the mundane. Change happens over time. Rome wasn't built in a day, and it will take longer than a few days to change a lifetime of habitually thinking in negative ways. I had to kill condemnation, or it was going to kill me. I was going to corner it and cancel it out before it canceled me out. Being battle-weary didn't matter because I would rather die than quit. I simply had to learn how to win the battle that was already won for me. But I often think that God leaves some enemies so He can teach our hands to war and our fingers to battle. He was making me a warrior; I just didn't realize it at the time.

Blessed be the LORD, my rock, who trains my hands for war, And my fingers for battle.

PSALM 144:1 NKJV

We must pray we can walk out what He has worked in us—as with any healing and deliverance, walking it out is the key. Getting free is one thing—staying free is quite another. Avoid both legalism and giving self a license to indulge. The wisdom is to stay away from the ditches on both sides. Avoid the extremes. We cannot rid ourselves of standards and goals and just cast off restraint. Nor can we bind ourselves to perfectionistic ideals and be a killjoy both to others and ourselves.

CONNECT 8

Here's an exercise that I did to help me change my brain. As my thoughts lined up, my emotions, though reluctant at times, followed suit. Since the obstacle was in my thinking, that had to change.

A mentor challenged me with a course of action. She was aware of how I often struggled with not necessarily knowing that God loved me, but more so with being continually aware that He loved me. She challenged me to set an alarm every eight minutes and to have it go off. Each time it went off, I needed to make a conscious effort to reconnect with God in my heart and thoughts, to become aware of His Presence and love for me. It was not her original idea, but one that she thought would help me.

I took the cognitive challenge. Talk about an interruption! To date, this had to be one of the most challenging things that I have ever done. This happened to be around the holiday season, and I did it for two weeks solid. It was intense, difficult, and I thought quite impossible at times. Literally, during all waking hours, every eight minutes, my alarm would sound or vibrate, and I would stop and focus on the truth that God loved me and that I was accepted. I also whispered my love and affection back to Him. We connected every eight minutes. I discovered later that eight means new beginnings.

At first, I was annoyed by the practice; however, I was determined to pursue this challenge aggressively. As obnoxious as it was, it was helping me get to know the beast within. You know the machine that drives you to perform. I definitely saw the kind of thoughts that were running around in my head. As the alarm would sound, I jotted down the thoughts and emotions in my mind. I noticed that many of these thoughts tended toward the negative: annoyance, anxiety over things I could not control, care-taking, criticism, defensive, disappointment, emotionally distant, duplicity, fault-finding, fear, frustration, hopelessness, impatience, insecurity, internal pressure, irritation, nit-picking, manipulation, perfectionism, people-pleasing, placating, punishing thoughts of self-judgment, resentment from obligations I had to keep, regret, rushed, self-reliant, shame, stress, striving and worry.

In truth, the alarm would interrupt all these negative thoughts over the next two weeks. I couldn't get into much trouble in my mind because every eight minutes, an annoying alarm intruded to remind me to take captive my thoughts. I had to refocus my thoughts. I had to set them above. It was becoming very easy to identify them. They couldn't hide behind busy activity, as they were being subjugated. They couldn't get very far down the road because I was turning them back toward the heart of God for me.

AS I BEGAN TO SUBJUGATE THEM, MY NEGATIVE THOUGHTS COULD NO LONGER HIDE BEHIND BUSY ACTIVITY

After about the first week of the Connect 8 practice, I noticed that my thoughts were becoming ones of contentment, joy, confidence, rest, peace, quietness, and security. I became very aware that I was loved and accepted. No longer did I feel driven or that I had to be doing something 24/7. Nor did I also feel an unrealistic standard of perfectionism. I could differentiate between the voice of the Father and the devil, the liar, so clearly. They were very distinct. What I thought were my thoughts simply were the enemy's thoughts. It astonished me. After a week of aggressively training my brain, not only were my thoughts lining up, but my emotions followed suit. It seemed almost too good to be true.

This exercise helped me to sort out the following:

1. **Recognize**—What am I thinking about?
   Where is the seat of my affection?

2. **Renounce**—What lies do I believe in
   that I need to renounce?

3. **Reconnect**—What is the heart of Father God toward me?

This continual exercise was the exact opposite of what I once knew. Where there once was a constant barrage of judgment, now I intentionally had a storehouse of affirming thoughts and positive images about my value and worth to God. It is work, and I had to reach for it. Some would say that it is too exhausting and hard. Admittedly, it was more of a challenge than at other times, but living as I did was harder. Is it difficult to change? Yes! Impossible? No! I was desperate to climb out of the pit of despair. If you choose to do this exercise, it will cost you time. View it as exchanging your time for His thoughts and ways.

None of us can operate beyond our character, and we must be bigger on the inside than the outside. This takes yielding and surrendering to God's will and way. It takes a pursuit of all we are, of God and His higher thoughts and ways.

I remember the day when I had to surrender the crutch of condemnation. It was similar to the day I turned in my victim card. There are some days where I inadvertently reach for it, but then I'm reminded by love that I don't need that crutch anymore. I may limp, but it is okay. The crutch of condemnation gave me permission to not possess the inheritance God had for me in the Promised Land. It made me content to live in the wilderness. After all, the manna fell every morning, the fire kept me warm, and the cloud moved when there was a change in direction. Of course, it wasn't ideal, but I had learned to manage (Exodus 16; 13:21, 22).

I am not going to lie to you. Anytime you see any Christian living in victory, you can make a note to yourself: *That is not an accident. That didn't just happen overnight.* It is with effort and cooperating with the spirit of grace that we can walk in the Spirit. It is easy to live a life governed by sense knowledge or the flesh. We literally have to do nothing. Passivity is the petri dish of mediocrity. But it is an entirely different matter to live a life following after the Spirit.

IT IS WITH EFFORT AND COOPERATING WITH THE SPIRIT OF GRACE THAT WE CAN WALK IN THE SPIRIT

9

AN ESSENTIAL TRUTH

And have clothed yourselves with the new [spiritual self],
which is [ever in the process of being] renewed and remolded
into [fuller and more perfect knowledge upon] knowledge
after the image (the likeness) of Him Who created it.

COLOSSIANS 3:10 AMP

A child doesn't have the ability on their own to develop a healthy sense of self but often searches for that identity from others and the world around them. Like anyone else, initially, my identity was in the wrong place. Not knowing who I was, I erroneously concluded that I was the sum of my experiences and the deficits that I carried through life. As a kid, due to many painful experiences, I felt inferior: less than, second-rate, not as good as, and shameful like I was an embarrassment. I wanted to apologize for being, and I often wished that I could erase myself. I lived in a continual comparison, where I always came up short. Constant bullying by the condemning thoughts often caused me to feel internally defensive.

Though I was riddled with insecurities on the inside, I was a bright, funny, and quick-witted child who could do things well on the outside. Academics came easy; I was athletic, articulate, favored, and well-liked. I was an Honor student, graduated fourth in my class, and absolutely loved school, but I felt like it was all a lie, and I was a fraud. I felt stupid; I just could not figure out why I could do the work. The internal tension was continually there to affect my responses and outlook on life. It was awkward to hear my name called for a reward or a trophy, but if it was not called, I felt devastated. It made no sense.

Change took some time. Recognizing and dealing with the source of the condemnation was critical, but other factors needed to come into play. Following my initial deliverance, I confess I was waiting for the familiar feelings to return. After all, I had received temporary relief from it before here and there. Then, I felt like something was constantly chasing me and that I had to try to stay ahead of it by doing things just right. The problem was, my humanity would show up, and everything I was running from would catch up with me. Running is exhausting work. The self-berating and deafening dialogue would begin again. Numerous encounters with the presence and the love of God, along with studying and understanding righteousness, are what finally brought about the permanent change within the framework of my mind.

UNDERSTANDING RIGHTEOUSNESS

My mom was at a yard sale and picked up a used book for a buck that she gave to me. She knows that I have a love for old books, and this one was well-worn from age and use. It was called *Two Kinds of Righteousness* by E.W. Kenyon. Little did I know the treasure this small book contained and how it would change my life!

Kenyon defined righteousness as the ability to stand in God's presence without the sense of guilt, condemnation, or inferiority. Concepts of not only being clothed in righteousness but actually partaking of the righteousness of Christ were things that made me hungry to know more. How was this possible? Though the words I was reading were foreign concepts to me, I consumed the book and could not put it down. These truths began to rock my world.

> RIGHTEOUSNESS IS THE ABILITY TO STAND IN GOD'S PRESENCE WITHOUT THE SENSE OF GUILT, CONDEMNATION, OR INFERIORITY

Incidentally, one of the first things that I noticed when I just started showing up and hanging out with God with no agenda other than to be with Him was that I began to learn about righteousness. Knowing that by believing and trusting in Jesus' finished work makes me righteous took on new meaning. It wasn't based on who I was, what I did, or how I felt and thought. Because of God's great heart and understanding, I could fearlessly, confidently, and boldly draw near to Him with freedom from fear and inferiority. I could receive grace. I could fall on His mercy, ask for help, and receive it for my failures. God and I could hang out without my having to be this perfect ideal me that didn't exist anyway and is never going to exist. I have made peace with that reality. This was a life-changing revelation.

OUT IN THE OPEN

I was not a prayer-less woman by any means, but something different was taking place. Slowly I was letting God in all the way. I abandoned myself to God; I wanted Him to wreck the life I thought

I controlled. Crazy prayers get crazy results. Rather than going to prayer and getting some things accomplished, I would just go and be with Him. Sitting in His presence, I would ask Him, "What is on your heart?" It turned out that I was on His heart. He needed to address some strongholds deep within me that kept me from the abundant life He desired for me.

There were times where God would break through with such a powerful love that left me weeping. His presence was like oceans of love washing over me. Those were moments where I would see God for who He really was, a loving and wonderful Papa. It was a dream come true, and I would cling to them. Those moments would leave me with a resolve that I absolutely refused to be defined by a handful of days in my life that did serious damage. I had to believe that God was big enough to break through my brokenness and do a miracle within.

> And not a creature exists that is concealed from His sight, but all things are open and exposed, naked and defenseless to the eyes of Him with Whom we have to do.
>
> Inasmuch then as we have a great High Priest Who has [already] ascended and passed through the heavens, Jesus the Son of God, let us hold fast our confession [of faith in Him].
>
> For we do not have a High Priest Who is unable to understand and sympathize and have a shared feeling with our weaknesses and infirmities and liability to the assaults of temptation, but One Who has been tempted in every respect as we are, yet without sinning.
>
> Let us then fearlessly and confidently and boldly draw near to the throne of grace (the throne of God's unmerited favor to us sinners), that we may receive mercy [for our failures] and

find grace to help in good time for every need [appropriate
help and well-timed help, coming just when we need it].

HEBREWS 4:13-16 AMP

These scriptures became a comfort to me. It stated that not a
creature could be concealed or hidden from His sight. To me that
meant, not even crafty condemnation! It is exposed, naked and
defenseless and stripped of its power. The key here is that we must
live in light and truth. We must come out from hiding and reveal
the things that threw us in the cellar of condemnation. His Word is
a sword that can destroy the creature(s) hidden below the surface.
Then the scriptures continue on to give a revelation of the heart of
Jesus. He understands, sympathizes, and has a shared feeling with
our weaknesses, infirmities, and our susceptibility to the assaults
of temptation. He has been there, but He didn't sin in it.

A SURE FOUNDATION

God building me with a fixed and firm foundation is what I am after.
He is my personal architect, builder, and maker.

For he (Abraham) was [waiting expectantly and confidently]
looking forward to the city which has fixed and firm
foundations, whose Architect and Builder is God.

HEBREWS 11:10 AMP

Realizing that God is making me according to His blueprint and
design set me free from many traps, especially comparison. I need
not compare my building with someone else's. I'm tailor-made by
the Master's design, so comparison to others is an exercise in futility.
Adopting this mindset alone destroys the trap of comparison. I
can be confident in what God is building and doing in my life and

celebrate the uniqueness of others without comparing. I am not supposed to be you and vice versa. We simply cheat the world and one another when we do not bring forward who and what we are. What we are is valuable. We are unique and not meant to be measured by one another. Comparison leads to condemnation or pride. Both are deadly ingredients that are best to avoid in our foundation. These were liberating thoughts.

That being true, I must be vulnerable to trust God when I don't understand, and when He doesn't let me in on the complete design. Some blueprints He will not show us as He deals with fault lines and cracks in our foundation that perhaps are not visible to anyone but Him. We must accept them and press forward with trust. I believe that God cares too much for us to allow progress too far into the journey before He orchestrates situations that allow Him to get our attention and deal with our broken places and mend us. He is a craftsman cultivating our character. We are in good hands.

EVERYTHING THE ENEMY WHISPERS IS A LIE Everything the enemy whispers is a lie. He's repeated the scenario with the same words throughout your life with many different people. But a lie is still a lie, and it is faulty material that cannot go in the building and making of you. I had to combat the lies with the truth while my emotions screamed the opposite. I persisted. The joy I saw in others, the way they enjoyed Father God in a childlike way, was intriguing. My motivating inward thought was, *I press on!*

Throughout my life, I've had encounters with God as the Bible came alive. His Word has been an anchor and what I've held onto when all looked lost. Often I said this to be true of myself, "All I am is a woman with a promise from God." I know deep within that

God cannot lie. Soaking in the truths of righteousness, the Father's unconditional love, and the blood of Jesus that heals, cleanses, and delivers were areas that became my mind's focus. As these truths began to resonate, they began to dislodge a lifetime of lies.

Finally, when the root of condemnation was dealt with, many things began to change. I was walking around enjoying the reprieve, but at the same time, kind of holding my breath. Yet, the days turned into weeks, and weeks into months, then months into years. It was still quiet and peaceful inside. Wow! Life was good on the other side. It felt as if I had this innermost secret on how good life was. It is liberating to be free from the driving, condemning thoughts. Who knew one could live like this? The only way I can describe it is that it was like living a dream!

The consistency of change was behind me. I had to learn to walk out my healing and build my faith. I now live in a place of peace. I remembered that when the noise inside my head was finally silenced, I felt a bit bored. Adjusting to this new normal took some time. This is not to say that this is the victory tour, and I no longer have to fight this battle. The difference is that I am now fighting the battle from without, not from within.

As the truth of righteousness and love gained ascendency in my life, condemnation began to dislodge. I would not trade my journey for anything. When I think of all that I learned about myself, Father's heart, and how to use the Word of God as an offensive weapon to walk out my healing and deliverance, it is astounding. It was my School of the Spirit. The Holy Spirit is a magnificent Teacher.

IF YOU LIVE IN CONTIUNOUS COMPARISON,
YOU WILL ALWAYS COME UP SHORT,
AND CONDEMNATION WILL RESULT.

BUT YOU ARE TAILOR-MADE BY THE
MASTER'S DESIGN, AND BECAUSE OF
GOD'S GREAT LOVE AND UNDERSTANDING,
YOU CAN COME BOLDLY AND WITHOUT
SHAME INTO HIS PRESENCE.

THE MORE YOU DO THIS, THE MORE
CONDEMNATION WILL DISLODGE, AND
YOUR FREEDOM WILL BE ASTOUNDING.

10

MOVING FORWARD

> Straightening up, Jesus said to her, "Woman,
> where are they? Did no one condemn you?"
> She said, "No one, Lord."
> And Jesus said, "I do not condemn you,
> either. Go. From now on sin no more."
>
> JOHN 8:10-11 NAS

After walking out my healing and deliverance for a season, I began to notice that my outlook on life was decidedly healthier. Discovering that perfectionism is an impossible feat and a lie freed me to approach life differently. I was done with chasing an illusion anyway. When has anything ever been perfect? It never has regardless of how hard I've tried. So I decided that no matter what the task was before me, I would attempt to do my best. Forget perfection. I can do my best and be excellent. I can have the spirit of excellence without being perfect. Perfectionism is not to be confused with being excellent. My motto became, "My best, God's glory!"

Not only was my outlook different, but the lies that usually rushed to the forefront of my mind were also countered immediately.

While I was at a corporate prayer meeting with a few people in attendance, a thought, *There is not enough prayer going on,* crossed my mind. Immediately, I heard God counter that thought with another: *The prayer is enough because I add My superabundant grace to it.* That changed my perspective instantly! God was not so concerned about numbers or the people's abilities. The truth is that His presence and ability in the activity were enough. That took the burden and the pressure off me. For it is by grace, not works. I felt confident that I was valued and accepted; this gave me the courage to ask God to separate the truth from the lies in me. It began to change the way I viewed life and ministered.

Here is an excerpt from my journal.

As I preached this morning, more of the love of God poured through, and the power of God was strong. There was deliverance happening everywhere. It was effortless as His Presence saturated the place. Needless to say, He poured me out. I prayed for around 40 people and was having fun with Father ministering. But this time—I was so aware of how emptied out I was.

I came home—(here's the different part) I took a bubble bath, lit a candle, and listened to anointed music, and just relaxed while He refreshed me. I was not driven to do more. An ability to rest just showed up. I had peace and was refreshed. This was a radical shift! I was free this time to do something different. I rested in a different way.

KEEPING IT SIMPLE

God can reaffirm His acceptance and love for us in unsuspecting ways. One day I felt led to read a children's book about Father God's love. It was part of a series of children's books by Max Lucado. The story is about a little person who messed up, and later stumbled into his maker, Eli's workshop. Instead of being condemned by his maker, he was told, "I love you because I made you. That's why you're special." The little guy was relieved because Eli wasn't angry with him and that his voice was calm, gentle, and kind. Afterward, I had to smile because God was reinforcing something deep within me with that story. Sometimes it's not what He says but how He says it that is healing and profound.

Besides God reaffirming His love for me through that simple story, I celebrated the fact that I was willing to read a children's book and let Him touch a place of need in my life. Initially, I felt embarrassed reading a child's book, but that day, it was exactly what I needed. I could relate to God differently and let Him meet those previously unmet needs in a healthy way. Too often, those areas of need drove me to the wrong place to try to meet my needs for acceptance or worth. Many of those decisions led to more pain and condemnation. Oftentimes in attempts to heal ourselves, we make things worse.

As with any healing and deliverance— walking it out is the key. We must pray we can walk out what God has worked out within us. It is imperative that we do not open doors again or break down hedges that are meant for our protection. Certain areas are best to steer clear from because they invite

OFTENTIMES IN AN ATTEMPT TO HEAL OURSELVES, WE MAKE THINGS WORSE

condemnation. There must be guardrails to prevent us from going over the cliff.

One of those areas for me is my response when I make a mistake. Dwelling on the mistake while I berate myself is not an acceptable response any longer. Quickly running to God's throne of grace and simply asking for help is the life-giving alternative. Then I release it, drop it, and let it go. The same thing applies if I sin. As soon as I recognize it or when the Holy Spirit convicts me about something, I humbly ask for and receive forgiveness. Whether the area is an attitude or action, my response to His conviction is quicker, and He immediately stops convicting me. I repent and correct it. Peace returns. I guard my peace as I have learned the Holy Spirit leads by peace. When I ignore Him, He continues to gnaw at me. My peace is disrupted as He is trying to get my attention to keep me walking in harmony with God. I have found the practice of ignoring Him and continuing in my disobedience eventually leads me into condemnation.

VALUE OF OBEDIENCE

Jesus frees us and enables us to live a life totally different than before. He always runs the accusers off, as He did with the woman caught in adultery, but He does clue us in to a truth—bad behavior will result in bad emotions. When I obey, even in a struggle, I live in peace. When I rebel, there is an instant war that ensues. If we have patterns of disobedience in our life, there will be condemnation if we do not heed to the conviction of the Holy Spirit and repent and be cleansed by the blood of Jesus.

We must believe what the Bible says and obey it. In Deuteronomy, we are told that the key to life is obedience. This comes with a promise that we will have life and peace. If we do not honor and obey God, we will have death and destruction.

"This command I am giving you today is not too difficult for you to understand, and it is not beyond your reach. It is not kept in heaven, so distant that you must ask, 'Who will go up to heaven and bring it down so we can hear it and obey?'

It is not kept beyond the sea, so far away that you must ask, 'Who will cross the sea to bring it to us so we can hear it and obey?'

No, the message is very close at hand; it is on your lips and in your heart so that you can obey it."

DEUTERONOMY 30:11-14 NLT

God wanted to make sure that the Israelites were clear about the consequences of their choices for themselves and their descendants. We are free to choose; however, we are not free from the consequences of our choice. There is no doubt that God always wants us to choose the way of life because it is the better way.

"Now listen! Today I am giving you a choice between life and death, between prosperity and disaster. For I command you this day to love the LORD your God and to keep His commands, decrees, and regulations by walking in His ways.

"If you do this, you will live and multiply, and the LORD your God will bless you and the land you are about to enter and occupy. But if your heart turns away and you refuse to listen, and if you are drawn away to serve and worship other gods, then I warn you now that you will certainly be destroyed.

"You will not live a long, good life in the land you are crossing
the Jordan to occupy. Today, I have given you the choice
between life and death, between blessings and curses.

"Now I call on heaven and earth to witness the choice
you make. Oh, that you would choose life, so that
you and your descendants might live! You can make
this choice by loving the LORD your God, obeying
Him, and committing yourself firmly to Him.

"This is the key to your life. And if you love and obey
the LORD, you will live long in the land the LORD swore
to give your ancestors Abraham, Isaac, and Jacob."

DEUTERONOMY 30:15-20 NLT

When God wants to grow us, He typically gives us an experience to expand our vessel. In my case, He began to speak to me of His love and wanted it to go beyond a nice philosophy. God desires relationship. We can keep the rules and still be laden with rebellion or we can learn how to live in the safety of obedience. God desires relationship; a real life lived before him motivated by love, not fear. We are sons and daughters, not orphans performing for His good favor and rewards. We get the goods because we are His kids. This is obedience motivated out of love rather than fear. Righteousness can't be legislated. If rebellion is in the heart, we can keep the rules and appear to be obedient, but the independency to operate outside of God is still deep within. Essentially, we are still living outside of where we are meant to dwell and occupy.

This truth bears repeating; demons drive. Remember what happened to the pigs that the demons entered after leaving the tormented man? (Matthew 8:30-32) They drove the pigs over a cliff to their deaths.

When I was in Israel, I was blessed to stop at this sight. It is thrilling to be on location where Jesus made the trip to free this tormented soul. I could not help but think of my own story and how Jesus made the journey to set me free. I am no longer driven by demons but led by peace.

Demonic imps are silenced from whispering in your ear because your mind has been trained to distinguish the lie. It is your time to rise up and decide that you're taking charge over your mind by the Word of God. Your moment is here to do your own thinking and experience transformation. His grace is present to help you.

MEASURING YOUR OWN PROGRESS

Usually, others can see our potential, but we only tend to see our pitfalls. Emotions of unworthiness and inadequacy are hurdles that we must jump over. Comparison and our own expectations probably do more to rob our joy than anything else. Paul was right when he said that it is not beneficial to compare ourselves among ourselves.

> For we dare not class ourselves or compare ourselves
> with those who commend themselves. But they,
> measuring themselves by themselves, and comparing
> themselves among themselves, are not wise.
>
> 2 CORINTHIANS 10:12 NKJV

No one is blessed at my expense. If God gives favor to another, it does not diminish His favor on me. God has more than enough blessing to go around. Yes, we all struggle; however, that does not mean comparing our lives to someone else's just to feel better is helpful either. External situations are not to be used as an excuse to sin continually. The Bible points right to the core of our problem.

It is what comes from inside that defiles you. For from within, out of a person's heart, come evil thoughts, sexual immorality, theft, murder, adultery, greed, wickedness, deceit, lustful desires, envy, slander, pride, and foolishness. All these vile things come from within; they are what defile you.

MARK 7:20-23 NLT

Do you see that? Evil thoughts! Condemnation is an evil thought, and it was defiling me from within. There is a big difference between fighting an enemy from within and one from without. I had battled the enemy in me for so many years that I was happy to turn the Holy Spirit loose inside. Some battles have been too bloody to give back to the enemy any ground gained. Don't let him have your hard-fought victories. The battle was too bloody. Make no time for regrets, regression, or retreat.

Here is a challenge for you—change your story or get a new one! Get rid of the crutch of condemnation. No longer identify with it. Open up to new possibilities. Do the scary stuff. You're not second rate; you are more than a conqueror in Christ. Do what God made you to do. Be who you are. You are an object of His love and affection; you are valuable. God doesn't find fault with you. Some of you relate to my story and beat yourselves up 24/7. You can stop. Remember, God is not mad at you. I believe it is on the heart of Father God to lift the lie of condemnation off of His children. God often leads me to minister along these lines to people in the meetings that I am in now.

CHANGE YOUR STORY OR GET A NEW ONE!

I make no claims to be a theologian. There are others more knowledgeable than I who could speak on this subject but, one claim I do make-- I have taken a ball bat to condemnation and by the grace of God, live in victory over it. Condemnation is a killer, and I have spent the majority of my life in its fierce battle. It crippled, contained, and constrained me. Fortunately, there is life after hell—it's called a Resurrection.

Living free from driving and condemning thoughts is exhilarating. My mind is free to meditate upon higher thoughts. Now I can think on God's thoughts and the visions that help and build people. Visions of teaching and learning from others, building schools, feeding the nations, and helping my neighbor now occupy my mind. There is now margin within to be creative. As these visions become reality, I do them with joy because I have been freed from this very draining battle.

Thankfully, I have learned the difference between conviction and condemnation. I can now take the Lord's correction without feeling condemned. It has made learning a far more enjoyable experience. I keep a close watch on a heart that tends to wander from grace and truth. As wise Solomon said, "Above all else, guard your heart, for everything you do flows from it" (Proverbs 4:23). If I've done something to offend or grieve God, I ask Him to forgive me. I think it is arrogant to never have to apologize in any relationship I am blessed to have, especially one with God. There is something about having confidence before God in unbroken, continual fellowship. I so enjoy His company, and He enjoys mine. It is more than I imagined, and I have so much to discover. So far, it has been an epic journey!

CONVICTION PUSHES US TO HIM.
CONDEMNATION DRIVES US AWAY FROM HIM.

IT IS HIS GRACE, NOT OUR WORKS THAT
MAKE US ACCEPTABLE TO GOD.

11

BEAUTY FROM THE ASHES

To console those who mourn in Zion,
to give them beauty for ashes,
the oil of joy for mourning,
the garment of praise for the spirit of heaviness;
that they may be called trees of righteousness,
the planting of the LORD, that He may be glorified.

ISAIAH 61:3 NKJV

It was a typical east coast winter, and I was headed to a weekend getaway at a favorite spot in Cape May, NJ. I love walking the shore, no matter the weather or season. There is something about taking a stroll and talking to Jesus while surrounded by such beauty. Earlier, I had written down on paper every condemning thought and act that I had been a part of and then burned them in the fire pit on my deck. The ashes were gathered into a tin and tucked away safely. Clutching the tin, I poured out my heart to God as I opened it, and I prepared to cast the ashes into the water. As I went to discard them, a gust of wind and waves consumed them, vanishing into the sea. It was as if they never existed. Right then,

I felt God's presence so strong ministering to me out of Isaiah 61. He assured me that He is totally capable of making all things new. Instead of shame, I will have double honor, and He will give me beauty for ashes.

Burning the papers bearing the condemning thoughts and acts, gathering the ashes, and throwing them away for me was a point of reference. In the process, I learned that we cannot keep ashes and obtain joy. Sometimes we have so identified with the ashes we do not want to release them but rather make a memorial around them. However, by letting them go, we have room for new promises.

OVERCOMING

Having battled condemnation for so long, I realized that, "Though it may not be my fault, it is my fight." Those words have become my motto when I minister on overcoming condemnation. I think it is a great day when we discover our fight. Don't battle on the wrong field, but when you find your enemy, become a warrior. Be as committed to his destruction as he is yours. Run to the battle. Fight the good fight of faith.

IT MAY NOT BE MY FAULT, BUT IT IS MY FIGHT!

I am particularly humbled during those times when we feel like we are getting kicked all over by the enemy, and God brings a victory. I realize all glory goes to Him. It is worth staying in the fight and going from glory to glory! After all, Jesus is fighting this fight with us, and He is undefeated.

I have this sense of urgency to help others recognize condemnation in their lives and kill it. Its effects leave us spiritually dwarfed and defeated. When I think of the love we forfeit due to this fierce foe, it saddens me. We miss out on a great love adventure with the Father. I don't want to live a moment outside of His love, especially when He paid such a price to give it to me. Why be content to live at a deficit? It is available to us to be loved and to be celebrated rather than tolerated.

It is sad when we opt for performing for God rather than playing with Him. It is easier to work for God than to be in awe at the wonder of who He is and who we are in Him. Sadly it is even easier to stay busy doing Kingdom work rather than to stop and get real. We must get real to get right. People who are lovers of God may not necessarily look like they are working, but I can assure you that worshippers accomplish more than the workers do. Lovers do labor, but what they do in prayer and in His presence trumps the work of mere human programs.

REBUILDING

We would all agree that it is not wise to associate with people who carry and cooperate with certain spirits such as legalism and criticism or those that are judgmental because we must be cautious with whom we build. You cannot build with people who are set to destroy you. The same is true in the building of our lives. The material that goes into the construction of our lives is crucial. Just as it is not wise to build with certain people, neither is it wisdom to be careless with the material you use to build your life. You are the foreman, build according to heaven's blueprints. If the foundation of your life is not enough to sustain the weight of what God wants you to carry, then eventually, what you build will come crashing down. Pressure exposes fault lines in the foundation. Address them.

What He destroys cannot be rebuilt.
JOB 12:14 NLT

God does a thorough job when it comes to delivering His own from the enemy. When God routs the enemy, it is over! God's liberating truth and my continual abiding in that truth have destroyed the condo of condemnation. I no longer dwell at that address.

> For if I build again the things I destroyed,
> I make myself a transgressor.
>
> GALATIANS 2:18 NLT

The no-judgment zone is where I now live. My position is from the place of truth, declaring that Jesus was judged in my place. Through Christ, I escaped God's wrath. I can continually live in the Father's love and acceptance of me by a constant awareness that I'm forgiven, and God is faithful to cleanse me from all sin and unrighteousness. I live free of condemnation and am only experiencing love and His acceptance.

God does speak to us. His ways are so much higher, and His thoughts so much greater. I desire to be more sensitive to His thoughts and become more aware of His Presence than any other competing factor. Now, I can't afford to think contrary to His truth of me. My desire is to adopt His loving attitude toward me and that I will have His attitude and heart towards others. Often what is wrong with our vertical relationship is our horizontal relationship. If I don't spend time in the vertical, I will never receive what I need to address in the horizontal.

Condemnation is a slow, driving death. Harboring judgmental, condemning emotions sabotages your mental health. Neglecting to deal properly with negative emotions can lead to depression. Addressing the spiritual aspect of it is imperative. That has been a primary focus of this book, but there are additional things that combat a possible descent into depression.

Being that we are also a physical man, we cannot run our bodies down and not expect adverse side effects. Some healthy outlets that address our physical needs are journaling, exercise, rest, proper nutrition, and vitamin supplements. I understand that I am responsible for my freedom. Part of that is taking care of my physical body, which is crucial in mental and emotional prosperity. It is not about being perfect but about caring for my physical body as a means to honor my temple, which houses the presence of God.

A COMPLETED WORK

I hope freedom comes to those reading this if you feel like God lives to find reproach with you. Jesus bore our condemning sentence. I believe God says to you, "Take the club out of your hand." Just as Jesus was whipped, it says in the Bible that they blindfolded Jesus, took a club, and bashed Him in the head and said, "Prophesy, Christ! Who did it?!" He could have told them who did it. But I believe that He stood there and took it because of people like you and me. Jesus knew that we would be bashed in the head almost daily with condemnation, and He took that beating so we could be whole in our minds, emotions, and in our person.

> Surely He has borne our griefs and carried our sorrows; Yet we esteemed Him stricken, smitten by God, and afflicted.
>
> But He was wounded for our transgression; He was bruised for our iniquities; the chastisement for our peace was upon Him, and by His stripes we are healed.
>
> ISAIAH 53:4, 5 NKJV

Jesus set us free so that we would stop picking on ourselves. He closed His mouth against His accusers so that we could open our mouth against the accuser of the brethren and rebuke him with the truth of "There is no condemnation to those who are in Christ."

You're going to feel the love of Father God, the love of Jesus Christ, your Savior, your Lord, and the love of the Holy Spirit, who is the Comforter. The Holy Spirit is actually the very sensitive side of God. Some people say it this way—He is the mother side of the heart of God. In Isaiah, it says He dandles His children upon His knees as a mother would. There's a very nurturing, tender, loving side to the heart of Father God (Isaiah 66:12-13).

God just wants to tell you that He loves you, and He doesn't find fault with you. He's not hard on you. He loves you and will not embarrass you. Come as you are and let Him fill you up. All that stuff that has bogged you down—the more you sit in God's presence, the more you are free from it. Imagine placing a vase with dried residue under a running faucet. In time, the flowing water will loosen it, bringing it to the surface so it can wash away down the drain. The vase is now clean.

Similarly, you just turn God on and let Him deal with the vessel. Simply stay there under His love and receive it, and you'll find yourself changing for the better. Things that you've tried for years to change begin to transform. You aren't merely better, you are new! You don't know how, because God does it.

I am grateful for the many tools in my arsenal: prayer, worship, fasting and fellowshipping with God around His Word. After all, Jesus is the lover of my soul, healer of my heart, and restorer of my mind. I believe that He will walk to hell and back with anyone brave enough to keep going. I also know that He loves us wherever we choose to stop. Personally, I've always wanted it all. Sometimes, I refer to myself as a God-hog. I want all of God that I can get and then some more. I love Him. Even in the decades of feeling that He only tolerated me, I still loved Him because somewhere deep within, I knew the problem was inside me and not with Him.

God and I have a history. It has been in my times of brokenness where my intimacy with Him was forged. I have had the privilege of leading many to Christ. I have seen miracles, and the hand of God operate throughout my life. Though I am grateful for those things, they have not compared to the hand of God touching my life, experiencing His Presence when I felt unloved, seeing His compassion, and discovering His heart. These are what motivate me to preach the Gospel to others. I serve an amazing Father, and I want others to know Him as I do. How Father God has handled me in my fragile state is why I love Him so. It is not when I am hitting the home run or the grand slam, but the times when God loved me when I felt unlovable. Who does that? An amazing dad does. God is for us and not against us. Put that in your foundation and build on bedrock, not shifting sand.

HOW FATHER GOD HAS HANDLED ME IN MY FRAGILE STATE IS WHY I LOVE HIM AS I DO

I hope to help others struggling in this area. I've overcome great adversity by the blood of the Lamb and the word of my testimony. Statistics shout that I should be something else, but my Savior said otherwise. I certainly make no claims to perfection, but I have learned how to implement principles and strategies successfully to combat it effectively. I have set my eyes on Him, His love for me, His acceptance of me, and the righteousness that Jesus died to give me shouts of my exquisite worth.

I pray you will take His scarred hand and get out of the pit of condemnation and journey to the Promised Land discovering the depths of the Father's heart.

GOD IS TOTALLY CAPABLE OF MAKING
ALL THINGS NEW—EVEN YOU,

EPILOGUE

Blessed are those who hunger and thirst for righteousness, for they shall be satisfied.

MATTHEW 5:6 ESV

Since first writing this book in 2014, much has happened. As with all truth, it is revealed to us in layers. The more we embrace it and walk in it, the deeper God takes us into the revelation. Because I am intentional to crush condemnation daily in my life, I find the things I desired for decades have fallen into place. There are times I reflect on the journey, and tears of gratitude stream down my face—overwhelmed and amazed at this life I get to live. I remember the depth of despair and depression He pulled me from as He taught me to cling to His promises.

The truth I now walk in has created opportunities that were previously elusive to me. Throughout my childhood, I thought victorious lives were slated for others but not for me. But as I walked through the process, He patiently taught me, and my life has emerged as an intrinsic brightly colored canopy displaying the epic tale of someone who wins more than they lose.

Even as I began to write this epilogue, feelings of awkwardness sprang up within tempting me to shy away from expressing such positive regard about myself. I then realized I am much more comfortable with sharing the struggle than I am in testifying about the blessing. I recognized the creepy voice of condemnation was at it again, accusing me of being braggadocios. It was a reminder that I am still on a journey of crushing condemnation. The truth is, doing the continual work presented in this book has resulted in a different life. It was work, but I enjoy the fruit of a life that is forever changed on the inside. However, it is a process.

I have been blessed with a wonderful husband, three amazing children, a son and daughter-in-love, two grandsons, faithful friends, health, and blessing, but there was a time when I could not sit still and enjoy the family gathered around me. Now I sit back, and I am able to take in the laughter around the holidays or summer vacations at the shore. Tears well up in my eyes because I am present in the moment. I am present to watch the sparkle in my grandsons' eyes as they discover something new. I am present to listen to the conversations over coffee and the discussions about current events. I am present, not just physically but emotionally and mentally. I am present and aware I now have the ability to rest in His blessing of family without being driven to perform.

> I CAN FINALLY BE FULLY PRESENT TO MY FAMILY—PRESENT AND AWARE—ABLE TO REST IN HIS BLESSINGS AND NOT DRIVEN TO PERFORM

I am astounded at the level of peace and blessing God has given me. He gave me rental property during a worship service. He told me to text the agent and make a ridiculous offer on two rentals. The guy took the offer for $20k less than the asking price. My income changed overnight. Financial blessing began to flow in a way that previously wasn't possible. When a person does not think they are worth much, typically financial blessing is something of which they feel unworthy. Yet, almost effortlessly, as my roots were being healed in the process, the fruit began to bear something different. I started to prosper; my family started to prosper; our ministry began to prosper. I obeyed God out of a mess, and it resulted in a blessed life. We cannot have negative thinking and a positive, joyful life. When I changed my thinking, everything around me changed.

When the Lord led us to purchase property for our ministry, the realization was beginning to sink in that even after months of negotiations and planning, the catering hall and restaurant space would not become the permanent home of our ministry. God's wonder was about to reveal itself once again. This time in the form of a simple phone call.

A Methodist church in our area (one with a 13,000 square foot building on five acres of land) was about to close its doors permanently and had heard about our plight on the local news. They called our office to inquire as to whether or not we'd be interested in a site visit and discussion since it was their preference to see another church carry on as stewards of the property. Less than twenty-four hours later, we were touring the facility with their retiring pastor and staff. After agreeing on a price during a short period of negotiation, and a time of due diligence, the ministry purchased the property in September of 2019.

God was with us and blessed us before a watching community. I am encouraging you to follow me as I follow Christ with feet of clay. I am a woman who became so desperate for freedom that I was willing to do what He led me to do in order to rid myself of condemnation and live the life Christ had called me to live. What I laid down opened to me opportunities to live a different life, to live at a different level, it attracted favor. It was a long process, but it was and is worth it.

Blessings overtake you as you step into covenant relationship. We are sons and daughters, and the blessings are rich. Relationally, we experience joy in family, in ministry, in life. Jesus came to give us abundant life. It has been many years walking out this truth, and I am happy to report the bottom hasn't fallen out. I give all glory and honor to Jesus. I am thankful. But make no mistake, God is no respecter of persons. What He did for me, He will do for you.

So, as you have read about my messy process, please keep in mind the fruitfulness of my life today. I am a different woman, and my life is completely changed. Only the grace of God could do that.

REFERENCES

Brown, Michael. *Go and Sin No More: a Call to Holiness.* Renew. 1999

Brown, Michael. *Hyper Grace.* Charisma House, 2014.

Hutson, Curtis. *Punchlines.* Sword of the Lord Publishers, 1990.

ABOUT THE AUTHOR

Teresa Verdecchio has a burden for people to experience the joy of being fully known and fully loved by God without shame, fear, or condemnation. She is a wife, mother, grandmother, mentor, author, and teacher. Pastor Teresa has co-labored with her husband, Dave, for over 30 years in ministry, reaching the hearts of men and women domestically and abroad. Together, they are committed to bringing hope to the hopeless, ministering the love of Christ through sound teaching, and tangibly expressing genuine compassion to see broken lives restored.

To learn more or to invite Pastor Teresa to speak at your conference or event:

TERESAVERDECCHIO.COM

Also from Pastor Teresa Verdecchio, *Praying in Tongues is Normal* is a book with a timely message for the Body of Christ. She has spent her life teaching the saints the benefits of praying in the Holy Ghost and equipping them to live victoriously through a life given to prayer. She has experienced first-hand the miraculous breakthrough and victory that comes from exercising this gift of the Spirit. Now more than ever, the people of God must use this powerful weapon to overcome in these perilous times. In this book, you will learn about the benefits of praying in tongues, receive sound biblical teaching on the different operations of tongues, and be equipped to walk with God at a greater level.

Made in United States
North Haven, CT
13 January 2022

14689359R00070